Ghosts & Haunted Houses of Maryland

Ghosts
&
Haunted Houses
of Maryland

BY TRISH GALLAGHER

Illustrated by Howard Burns

Tidewater Publishers

CENTREVILLE, MARYLAND

To my husband Dan, who never believed in my ghosts but always believed in me, and to my brother Tony, who always liked a good ghost story

Library of Congress Cataloging in Publication Data

Gallagher, Trish, 1958–
    Ghosts & haunted houses of Maryland.

    1. Ghosts—Maryland. 2. Haunted houses—Maryland.
I. Title.   II. Title: Ghosts and haunted houses of Maryland.
BF1472.U6G35 1988   133.1′09752   88–2163
ISBN 0–87033–382–8

Manufactured in the United States of America
First edition, 1988; seventh printing, 2007

Contents

Ghosts & Haunted Houses of Maryland

Preface

Maryland is "alive" with the dead—ghosts, haunted houses, and things that go bump in the day as well as the night. This is a collection of twenty-five of the most fascinating accounts of the supernatural in the state, presented almost entirely from a historical perspective. From the flatlands of the Eastern Shore to the mountains of western Maryland, from the hectic pace of the state's suburban areas to the leisurely life on the old tobacco plantations of its southern counties, you'll read ghost tales that are as varied as Maryland's geography. You'll meet characters like the infamous slave kidnapper, Patty Cannon, and the controversial Dr. Samuel Mudd. You'll visit the home which the anguished Mary Surratt refuses to leave, even in death, and tour a college frequented by some visitors who have been dead for over a century.

Ghosts & Haunted Houses of Maryland is the culmination of a year's worth of interviews with scores of people and research at virtually every main county library and historical society in the state. The collection is for "believers" and "nonbelievers" alike, and the accounts are true insofar as many of the people interviewed believe them to be true. The purpose of this book is neither to support nor to deny the existence of the supernatural, but rather to entertain and educate. Most importantly, the book should be seen as a combination of entertaining tales and historical fact written to provide

Ghosts & Haunted Houses of Maryland

a unique way of looking at the Maryland of yesterday and today.

There are a number of people without whose help I would not have been able to write this book. First and foremost are the individuals who kindly consented to share their stories with me. I walked away from all my interviews with these people feeling as though I'd made new friends. I would also like to thank the countless librarians, historical society members, and ghost tale collectors who led the way to much of the information I needed. Lastly, I would like to thank my husband Dan, who gave me the idea for this book.

His Name Was Mudd

At four o'clock in the morning on April 15, 1865, there was a knock on the door of the Mudd farmhouse in Charles County, about three miles from Beantown. Dr. Samuel Mudd, asleep with his wife Sarah in one of the upstairs bedrooms of their two-story home, awoke and went downstairs to see who was at the door. Little did Dr. Mudd suspect that that knock would change the course of his life. It would also introduce one of the most controversial points in American history—the question of Dr. Mudd's complicity in the assassination of President Abraham Lincoln.

On that morning in April, Dr. Mudd opened his front door to find before him two men, one of them badly in need of medical attention. It was the doctor's decision to extend his services and hospitality to the two men, thus forever entangling himself in the complex web of fact and fiction enveloping the murder of President Lincoln. Although Dr. Mudd later admitted to having met one of the two visitors, John Wilkes Booth, at an earlier date, he claimed that that April morning he had not recognized him or his companion, David Herold, both of whom were wearing makeshift disguises. Booth, his leg broken in his jump from the balcony of Ford's Theater to its stage, and Herold were taken in by the doctor. Dr. Mudd administered to Booth's leg and housed both the men until the afternoon of the same day. Both of them left the house between two and four o'clock on horseback heading toward Zekiah Swamp, allegedly without ever having revealed either their identities or their most recent activities.

Several days later, Dr. Mudd was taken into custody for his suspected role in the Lincoln assassination. He was tried and convicted by a military court and sentenced to life imprisonment at Fort Jefferson on Dry Tortugas Island, Florida. There he remained until his pardon by President Andrew Johnson over four years later, following a request for the doctor's release that had been signed by all the prisoners and wardens in appreciation for Mudd's aid in a yellow fever epidemic on the island.

Dr. Mudd returned to his home in March 1869 and attempted to reconstruct his shattered life, but never regained his health. He died in 1883, a man whose life and reputation had been irrevocably damaged by a decision one early spring morning to help two strangers.

Historians to this day disagree on the question of Dr. Mudd's complicity in the Lincoln assassination plot. It is known, however, that Mudd was a Southern sympathizer, as were many of his southern Maryland neighbors, and it is known that federal authorities were anxious to identify and condemn anyone even vaguely suspected of having had a part in the president's murder. In any case, Dr. Mudd's strongest supporters have always been his family members, who have sought to clear the family name for almost 100 years. The Mudds' efforts to remove the slur from their name have been successful to the point that even another U.S. president, Jimmy Carter, publicly proclaimed belief in the doctor's innocence.

Louise Mudd Arehart, the youngest grandchild of Dr. and Mrs. Samuel Mudd, has done the lion's share of the work toward re-establishing the integrity of the Mudd name. Most of Mrs. Arehart's efforts have been devoted to restoring and preserving the Mudd farmhouse for visitors as a site of national historic significance—efforts prompted by the ghost of her grandfather.

According to Mrs. Arehart, she had always been interested in her family's history and in the idea of preserving the farmhouse,

particularly since she was the last child born in the circa 1830 homestead. It was almost twenty years ago, Mrs. Arehart remembers, that the strange occurrences in her own house in La Plata, the Charles County seat, commenced. She began hearing knocking at the front door, but whenever she went to open it she found no one there. The sound of footsteps going up the stairs and down the hall was likewise not uncommon. Soon, Mrs. Arehart began to catch glimpses of a man on the grounds of her house. The man was always dressed in black trousers and vest, with a white shirt, its sleeves rolled up to the elbows. But she could never see his face clearly. After that, Mrs. Arehart recalls actually finding the man in the house one day while she was putting away silverware. She almost ran into him as she was going through the doorway to the dining room and they ended up passing each other. Startled, she took her dog throughout the house to check all of the rooms and closets for signs of the disappearing man but was unable to find him.

A week passed, and Mrs. Arehart was mentally reviewing the incidents involving the strange man. Suddenly, she realized that that man was no stranger to her—he was her grandfather, Dr. Samuel Mudd. Slowly, the pieces began to come together. There was a reason why her grandfather had returned and Mrs. Arehart believed that it concerned the state of his old home. The house had remained in the Mudd family over the years but had fallen into a sad state of disrepair. At that time it belonged to Mrs. Arehart's brother, Joe, who still farmed the acreage surrounding it. His sister was convinced that Dr. Mudd had returned in order to prompt someone to save the farmhouse, and she persuaded her brother to let it be turned into a museum that could eventually be opened to the public. Mrs. Arehart then began writing to senators and congressmen and organized the Committee for the Restoration of the Samuel A. Mudd House. As a result of her efforts, the house was listed on the National Register of Historic Places in 1974 and was opened to the public in August 1983.

Restoration of the old home is still not complete. At this writing, the kitchen is undergoing restoration and Mrs. Arehart has plans for several of the outbuildings. Having devoted so much of her time and energy to restoring her grandfather's home, Mrs. Arehart hopes that he is pleased with what she has done. She says, however, that she has to be careful to maintain a busy schedule aimed at completing restoration of the farmhouse, for when she slows down her grandfather has a habit of coming around and "bothering" her. In any case, it can certainly be said that Dr. Mudd's ghostly intervention has proved successful in preserving a piece of American history.

The Spirits
of Mount Saint Mary's

Few would imagine that a hectically paced college campus would be a likely environment for ghostly visitors, who are more often thought to prefer lonely, secluded locations and quiet surroundings. The spirits of Mount Saint Mary's, however, are a social bunch, and evidently the presence of over 1,400 students and teachers provides a stimulating atmosphere for the nonliving as well as the living.

Mount Saint Mary's is the oldest independent Catholic college in the United States. Founded in 1808 by Rev. John Dubois, a French emigré priest, it is nestled alongside the Catoctin Mountains about twelve miles south of Gettysburg, Pennsylvania, in Emmitsburg, Frederick County. Steeped in history as a result of its proximity to many Civil War battlefields, the 1,300-acre campus is also renowned for its association with Mother Elizabeth Seton, the first American saint, who made her home in the area and was responsible for founding the Sisters of Charity.

One of Mount Saint Mary's frequent visitors, according to the accounts of at least a dozen people in recent years, has been the alleged ghost of Rev. Simon Bruté, the first spiritual director of Mount Saint Mary's Seminary and a former president of the college. Rev. Bruté, who died in 1839, is said to have been seen walking the campus grounds in his flowing black robes, oftentimes tagging along behind a group of students. Witnesses tell of seeing this cassocked figure, with very distinctive facial features and deeply sunken cheeks, greeting people with a smile and a nod, and hurrying on to some unknown destination. Separate sightings of Rev. Bruté have been recounted by individuals who were able to describe his face and figure in great detail despite the fact that there is no picture of him anywhere on campus save for the college archives, which are not accessible to students.

The campus is said to be home to another ghost, this one the tortured spirit of a Confederate soldier who died at Gettysburg. Legend has it that the young soldier was engaged to be married just prior to his departure for the North, and that he sought to reassure his fiancee of his safety by picking out a star which would be their star. The youth told his fiancee that as long as they could both look up and see that star at night, they'd always be together. When the soldier was later killed in battle, the story continues, his body was one of several which did not receive proper burial at the hands of those employed to perform the job. The body of the young soldier was instead tossed—facedown—into an old well. According to student witnesses, the unhappy spirit of the Confederate soldier walks the campus grounds at night, seeking an end to his misery. On a number of occasions, students claim to have felt someone tap them on the shoulder from behind while they were walking through the campus at night. The shoulder-tapper has also been known to say, "Turn me over." Whirling around to investigate, students allege that they've never found anyone there. An interesting sidenote to this ghost tale is the historical accuracy of at least a part of the story. There are records that indicate that a man in the Emmitsburg area was prosecuted shortly after the Civil War for having failed to properly bury the bodies of some soldiers who had fallen in a nearby battle, a job he had been hired to do. The man was found guilty of having stuffed the bodies down a well.

Mount Saint Mary's also has a resident poltergeist, said to inhabit a dormitory room in one of the college's older buildings. According to Rev. Daniel Nusbaum, director of the school's Visual and Performing Arts Department, the reports of strange activities in room 252 have been frequent since he himself stayed in it eighteen years ago, before it was converted to a dorm room. Rev. Nusbaum tells of one corner of the room where it was impossible to put anything. Many were the nights when he'd carefully push the room's large, heavy bed into the corner before going to sleep only to discover upon awakening in the morning that the bed had been moved, with him in it, a foot or more away from the walls. Rev. Nusbaum also recalls the high incidence of articles being moved in the room—objects placed in one location would later be found on the floor or in another place altogether. The room's mysterious forces do not stop there, according to another of the priest's accounts. One night, he remembers, a student came to visit him in room 252 with the intention of teaching him how to play poker. Much to the student's dismay, however, Rev. Nusbaum succeeded in grasping the fundamentals of the game very quickly—despite the student's secretly marked cards. Thoroughly exasperated at his inability to win a hand, the student asked his partner how he could be faring so well when he had never even played before. Rev. Nusbaum admitted that for some strange reason he had been able to know every card the student had held in his hand. He opined that this uncanny ability probably had something to do with the room, which had already evidenced strange powers. The student was not convinced by his host's explanation until Rev. Nusbaum promised to show him that the room truly was a special one. He predicted that in fifteen seconds his cat would suddenly rise up on its haunches from where it had been resting peacefully on a nearby desk, arch its back, appear to stare at something in the corner of the room, and, just as suddenly, rush out of the room. Fifteen seconds passed. The cat abruptly sprang to its feet, arched its back, fixed an intense stare in the direction of the corner, and ran away. The cat's actions were repeated shortly thereafter by the now-convinced student, who failed only to arch his back before leaving. Rev. Nusbaum was left alone to ponder the oddity of both his remarks (for which he still lacks explanation) and his room.

The room has lost few of its peculiarities over the past years and students living in it have continued to report the strange properties which objects in the room seem to acquire. Tests conducted on the room have never revealed any evidence of vibrations or other natural phenomena that might explain the room's "haunted" behavior. Investigations regarding the history of the room, however, may provide some insight. According to Rev. Nusbaum, a priest who used to live in the room actually died in it. He was found one morning in a chair in the very corner of the room where it is impossible to keep furniture.

The Once and Haunted
Frenchtown Tavern

Located in Cecil County about three miles south of Elkton along the Elk River is Frenchtown, a port of significance for the state of Maryland over a century ago. Frenchtown's road to New Castle, Delaware, a popular way to travel between Baltimore and Philadelphia, was used by many stage or wagon travelers as the land part of their journeys to either Maryland or Pennsylvania. Frenchtown was badly damaged by the British in the War of 1812, but Frenchtown Tavern, a large brick structure built around 1800 and used as a public inn, survived the war.

Today, Frenchtown and its tavern are no more, but Mildred Alagia of Elkton fondly remembers the day over forty years ago when she and her husband decided to purchase the mansion, its farm and tenant houses, and the 300-odd acres of land that went with it. The property had been put up for sale in 1944 by an old gentleman from Philadelphia whose granddaughter had drowned in the river in front of the tavern. Said to have never recovered from the tragedy, the owner had decided to have nothing more to do with it. Somewhat overwhelmed by the idea of purchasing such a substantial piece of property, Mrs. Alagia nevertheless gave in to her husband, who had set his heart on owning Frenchtown Tavern.

According to Mrs. Alagia, the first sign anyone in the family had that all was not normal with the old mansion was observed before the Alagias moved in. Mrs. Alagia and her daughter Mary were in the basement. The two had decided to take a look at the original kitchen and were happily immersed in an inspection of the old stove and brickwork when the room suddenly turned extremely cold. A strange "whirlwind" seemed to form, growing in intensity until it was sweeping up dirt and small debris and twisting them in the air. The two women couldn't get out of the basement fast enough.

Once, a group of workers came from Philadelphia to lay carpet. The workmen had been told by the Alagias that, as a matter of convenience, they could spend the night in the still-uninhabited house. From all accounts, the workmen got something less than a peaceful rest in the old tavern. They later complained that they had been kept awake by the sounds of footsteps and rattling chains. They refused to stay another night at Frenchtown Tavern.

Although the Alagias had originally dismissed the ghost stories they had heard about their home, they soon came to give them greater credence as more family members experienced ghostly manifestations. One daughter, Rose, heard such loud talking and laughter one day while she was alone in the house on the second floor that she started down the steps to the first-floor living room to investigate. As soon as she reached the landing between the two floors, all of the sounds suddenly ceased. She was unable to find anyone in the living room or anywhere else in the house, for that matter.

Another daughter, Loretta, had a considerably more frightening experience. Walking up the stairs between the first and second floors, she saw a hand appear on the stairway. The strange hand grabbed the girl's ankle, forcing her to fall forward onto the steps. Unable to release herself from the mysterious fingers, Loretta screamed for help. As soon as other family members came to her side, the hand disappeared as inexplicably as it had appeared. No one was ever able to account for either its appearance or the bruises it left on Loretta's ankle.

Another episode which rivaled the ankle-grabbing in terms of sheer scariness occurred one evening when the family was in a second-floor sitting room watching television. After an extraordinarily loud noise caused them to jump in surprise, a look at the bedroom from which the noise had appeared to come revealed disturbing evidence of a supernatural nature. A crucifix on a wall over the bed had been ripped off its hanger and apparently thrown across the room.

Other strange things about Frenchtown Tavern included a bizarre cold spot on the third floor which everyone seemed to notice, and the sighting by Alagia grandchildren of a man in a uniform whom they called "the gray man."

Despite the fact that some of the Frenchtown incidents were frightening, Mrs. Alagia says that no one in the family ever felt threatened by any of the tavern's invisible guests. Although a clear explanation of the supernatural activity was never found, there were some oddities about the property which may provide a clue to solving its mysteries. A secret, windowless room was discovered by the Alagias in the tenant house. The room may have been used to hide slaves escaping north to freedom. There is another local legend that a boat full of slaves burned on the Elk River in front of the tavern with the loss of all the slaves, who could not escape from their chains. Unfortunately, the secrets of Frenchtown Tavern will never be revealed. Two fires, the first probably started by a faulty furnace, the other by kids playing around, completely destroyed the house in the 1960s.

The Cooking Ghost of
Ellicott City

Today the old Hayden house, or Oak Lawn as it was once known, is difficult to find, for its small granite structure has been almost completely surrounded by additions made to the old Ellicott City Courthouse. Built in the early nineteenth century, Oak Lawn was the residence of the first county clerk of the Howard County court, Edwin Parsons Hayden, who lived there with his wife and six children until his death in 1850. Thereafter, the house was occupied by several owners, including the Howard County Board of Education and the Howard County District Court. Vacant since 1981, it will soon begin a new life as the law library for Howard County.

Stories of the old Hayden house and its mysterious activities reached their peak in the 1970s when it was occupied by the district court and the county office of parole and probation. Clerks and secretaries would become spooked by such annoyances as lights that persistently turned on and off for no reason, an office coffeepot that would heat while remaining unplugged, and the sound of footsteps. The experience most common to the building's workers was smelling the aroma of soup wafting its way through halls and doorways, along with the occasional scent of bacon and eggs being prepared in the morning. The odors, which even occurred in the middle of the night, did not arouse considerable concern in and of themselves, but their source did cause some anxiety. There were never any cooking appliances in use in the old building and no cooking was ever done there by its occupants. Soon, the invisible chef was dubbed "the cooking ghost" and most of the visible inhabitants came to expect the occasional wave of kitchen smells.

For some people, however, the thought of having to work overtime hours unnerved them because it meant that they would be in the building after dusk and for the most part alone. They remembered too vividly the story of the rocking chair in one man's office that had been seen rocking by itself. They also remembered how the same person, arriving for work particularly early one morning, had glimpsed through the glass door panes the partial form of a man in the building. When the door to the building was unlocked and the premises searched, the man was never found.

Mr. Smith (not his real name) spent ten years working in the Hayden house and can still recall with great detail events that occurred during the late hours he often worked alone as the district court commissioner. Once, Mr. Smith had to take a quantity of cash to the Hayden house from another building where he had been collecting fines. At about four in the morning, Mr. Smith entered the building to use the safe. As he was turning its combination, he heard a noise behind him and stopped. He went out into the hall and looked around. There was nothing to be seen. Then, as he stood there, the door to the storage room next to him slowly swung open. However, there was no one behind the door. So unnerved was he by his experience that to this day Mr. Smith can't remember whether he ever did put the money in the safe or whether he took it back to the other building.

Another evening Mr. Smith was in his office working late. It was about one or two o'clock and he was alone in the building. It was a warm night and he had turned on the air conditioning. An extra table had been brought into his office earlier in preparation for an office party to be held the next day. As Mr. Smith sat at his desk, he noticed that a large stack of neatly folded napkins on the table had slowly started unfolding against the air current from the nearby air conditioner. Mr. Smith watched steadily as three napkins were carefully unfolded and then just as carefully refolded.

Only on one occasion did Mr. Smith see anything vaguely resembling a ghost. Working late again one night, Mr. Smith was on his way up to the second floor and had stopped at the landing before continuing his ascent up the next four steps. As he did, he noticed a cloud of white smoke out of the corner of his eye. It seemed to hang like a misty ball of vapor over the stairway. Although it was dense, he could see the wall behind it. When he turned his head slightly to give it a better look, the cloud had vanished.

Although Mr. Smith probably witnessed more manifestations in the old Hayden house than anyone else because of the late and solitary work hours he often kept, he never let his experiences bother him. He explained, "When you're dealing with criminals and drunks, ghosts are the least of your worries. I was always much more concerned about what a living person might do to me than a dead one."

Lilburn

Ellicott City seems to be a favorite spot for visitors from the beyond. Because its living residents have striven to retain the town's historic character, perhaps the dead feel a special affinity for the area: In addition to Oak Lawn, there are at least three other haunted houses in the downtown area of Ellicott City and three more on the outskirts.

Lilburn, one of the most beautiful old homes in Ellicott City, is also one of the town's most notorious haunted residences. The unexplained happenings within its granite Gothic style walls have given rise to ghost stories that date back to over half a century ago. Sited on eight acres of land overlooking the town's historic district, the twenty-room mansion was built by Henry Richard Hazelhurst in 1857. Mr. Hazelhurst was a prosperous businessman who made a fortune during the Civil War through his dealings in iron. As the years passed, a series of tragedies struck at Lilburn as Mr. Hazelhurst suffered the loss of his wife Elizabeth and several of their children, one of whom, a daughter, is said to have died in childbirth at Lilburn. Mr. Hazelhurst outlived many of his family members by a number of years. He died in 1900 at the age of eighty-five.

In 1923, the John Maginnis family purchased Lilburn and it was during this family's residence that rumors of ghostly activities in the mansion began to circulate through town. Footsteps were heard by the family in the tower, a massive structure abutting the back of the house. Other odd noises abounded, yet no one could determine the cause. Some people began to talk of the return of the Hazelhurst daughter who had spent her last living days at Lilburn before succumbing to her fate during childbirth. Tragedy almost visited Lilburn again when a Christmas tree in the living room caught fire. The fire quickly spread throughout the house, and although there was no loss of life, much of the old mansion was ruined. The house was reconstructed and the tower (which had been destroyed in the fire) was rebuilt with one major alteration to its original architecture—Mr. Maginnis replaced its Gothic peaks with parapets. This structural change seemed to cause an increase in the amount of ghostly activity at Lilburn and there were more than a few people who believed that the unhappy spirit of Henry Richard Hazelhurst had returned to protest the alterations.

Stories of the Lilburn ghost continued throughout the years, as the old house was successively owned by several different families. In the 1960s, it was purchased by the Sherwood Baldersons, who often related their experiences with Lilburn's supernatural inhabitants. The unexplained sound of footsteps was still a common phenomenon and the Baldersons' dog was reportedly afraid to go near a small room off the second-floor hallway. Additionally, the casement style windows in the tower rooms would not stay shut, prompting Mr. Balderson at one point to try to tie the windows closed with a heavy rope from the inside of the house. By the time he had finished tying the rope and descended to the outside of the mansion to inspect his handiwork, the ropes had already been loosened and the windows opened by unseen hands. On another occasion, a crystal chandelier in the dining room swung back and forth a number of times during a dinner party the Baldersons were giving for several of their friends. The diners were understandably alarmed at the unexplained behavior of the chandelier, particularly because there was no breeze in the area to account for the movement. A housekeeper for the Baldersons claims to have heard the sound of a child crying, to have smelled the heavy scent of a gentleman's cigar in the downstairs library, and to actually have encountered the forms of several ghosts during her tenure at Lilburn. Once, the housekeeper reported, the shape of a man seemed to bar her way into a room and she was compelled to push her way past him. Another time, she saw the figure of a pretty girl in a chiffon dress moving along one of the hallways.

Following the Baldersons, Dr. Eugenia King bought Lilburn and lived in the house with her son Jeff. She, too, reported problems with keeping the tower windows closed as well as repeat performances by the dining room chandelier and, on one occasion, a vase of flowers suddenly and inexplicably emptying itself out.

In 1983, Lilburn became the home of yet another family, the Whitneys, who moved in with their sons. Mrs. Julie Whitney admits that the house looked frightening when they first saw it, but she blames it on the dismal state of disrepair it had been permitted to fall into rather than on any supernatural causes. The Whitneys spent considerable time and effort restoring Lilburn to its former splendor, but failed to provoke any grumblings among its alleged invisible occupants. No one in the family has ever experienced anything strange in the house and, according to Mrs. Whitney, they don't expect to.

At the time of this writing, Lilburn is once again up for sale. The great house comes complete with a five-room guest house, an in-ground swimming pool, carriage and smoke houses, and however many ghosts may still be in residence. A fine opportunity to invest in a piece of the past—and the supernatural.

The Poltergeists of
Lawyers' Hill

Just east of Ellicott City in the
northeasternmost part of Howard County is the town of Elkridge,
once a bustling center of Maryland's early shipping industry. Some
lovely houses that were built in Elkridge's glory years still stand as
reminders of a more elegant time. Many of these fine homes are
concentrated in the wooded area of Lawyers' Hill; one of them is
said to house, at the least, a mischievous poltergeist.

The Lawn, as the large, two-storied house is named, was built
in the mid-1830s by Judge George Dobbin as a summer cottage and
retreat from the city heat of Baltimore. Judge Dobbin's home was
one of three built by lawyers in the immediate area—thus the name
Lawyers' Hill. Judge Dobbin eventually moved to The Lawn per-
manently for health reasons, and over the years the cottage acquired a number of additions, each indicative of a different archi-
tectural style popular to the period. The judge also added his own
skylights as well as an observatory for the pursuit of one of his
favorite hobbies.

In 1951, Mr. and Mrs. Joe Cobb purchased The Lawn from the
last of the Judge's descendants and over the next thirty-odd years
became convinced that they were not living alone in the house.
Doors locked and unlocked by themselves, and the key to the old
grandfather's clock, kept on a nearby shelf, would disappear and reappear without known cause. Once, a head of lettuce shot straight

up into the air over a table where Mrs. Cobb was preparing dinner. Strange events were not limited to the big house alone for two smaller houses or "tenant cottages" were also plagued by the mysterious. Tenants often complained of toilet paper either missing from the houses or removed from their bathroom holders.

Mr. and Mrs. Richard Menear, who rented the upstairs of the main house for a year, were also subjected to pranks, according to Janice Menear. One night, as the couple were in bed, they both heard an odd scraping noise which sounded as though some newly erected wall shelves in the kitchen were slowly being shaken out of their places. Upon investigating, the Menears could not discover anything amiss with the shelves, but both heard several other scraping noises issuing simultaneously from different areas of the house. They could find no explanation for the noises and returned to their room, where, Janice says, they "lay shivering for some time under the bedcovers." Locking doors seemed to be a favorite for the invisible prankster or pranksters. A hook-and-eye lock to the front door of the upstairs apartment was often found in place although the door was always kept open by the residents. On another occasion the key to a bedroom cupboard where Janice stored her cosmetics was stuck in the locked position. All attempts to turn the key and reopen the cupboard proved useless and it stayed locked for a month, until the day she stood before it with a hacksaw in her hand, ready to saw it open. Magically, a last try to turn the key was successful. Another time, an attic windowpane was found broken. Strangely enough, it looked as though it had been broken from the inside, not the outside, and no one in the house had done it. Still another time, Janice found her carefully planted windowbox flowers pulled up by their roots by some unknown weeder and meticulously arrayed side by side on the window ledge.

One of The Lawn's tenants reportedly used a Ouija board at one point to try to get to the bottom of the pranks. The board allegedly indicated that there were a number of spirits haunting all three of The Lawn's buildings. Something that may lend credence to this is an account by Janice of an incident involving a couple and their children who had lived in the main house. One night the family called numerous times to their six-year-old son, who was in his bedroom, to come to dinner. Exasperated after the boy had ignored their calls by answering that he was "busy," the parents went to his room to get him. There they found him sitting on his bed, as though engrossed in conversation with someone. The boy said, "Don't bother me. I'm busy talking to these people." When asked what people he meant, the boy rattled off the names of people who were later found to have been former occupants of The Lawn.

Ten years after their one-year residence, the Menears returned to Elkridge and purchased The Lawn from Mrs. Cobb, who had decided that it was too much for her to keep up with. Janice and her husband had always loved the house, and, ghosts or no ghosts, they had returned to make it their home. So far, she says, pranks have been kept to a minimum and she can recall only several odd things happening since their return. She was one day surprised to find a newspaper dated the exact day they moved into the house in back of an old hall closet she was cleaning out months later. Another time, a key that was kept in the keyhole of the library door was discovered missing. The two Menear children, Ian Paul, eight, and Jessica Brie, six, had been playing in the library one afternoon. When their mother went downstairs she found the library empty, the key gone, and the door locked. The key was later found, but the children claimed that they had not touched the key or locked the door. The key now hangs high on a wall by the library and no further mischief with the library door has occurred.

Although the Menears' son insists on sleeping with his light on at night, the rest of the family members do not let themselves be bothered by the ghostly occupants they may be sharing their home with. As Janice Menear puts it, "I just accept them as being there."

Ghostly Guests at
Mount Airy Plantation

Ghosts are not on the menu at Mount Airy Plantation although some staff members would insist that they should be, for traditionally they are as much a part of the bill of fare as the plantation's fine food.

Home of Maryland's famous Calvert family until 1903, Mount Airy was built in Upper Marlboro in southern Prince George's County around 1725. History has it that an earlier part of its structure had once served as a hunting lodge in the seventeenth century for the Lords Baltimore. In any case, the plantation, along with 9,200 acres of land, was a gift to Benedict Calvert from his father Charles, the fifth Lord Baltimore, in 1751. A little over twenty years later, George Washington crossed its threshold when arriving for a two-week wedding celebration of the marriage between his stepson John Parke Custis and Eleanor Calvert. Washington was not an infrequent visitor to Mount Airy, for he was a close friend of the Calverts. There are numerous references in his personal diary to his stays at the estate.

Our first president was not the only U.S. president to enjoy the fine hospitality offered at the stately home. Converted into a restaurant at the turn of the twentieth century after its sale to Matilda "Tillie" Duvall, Mount Airy was also visited by Presidents Hoover, Taft, Coolidge, and Wilson. In 1931, the home was again sold, this time to Eleanor "Cissy" Patterson, then editor-publisher of the

Ghosts & Haunted Houses of Maryland

Washington *Times-Herald*. Mrs. Patterson was responsible for making the last restorations (the house had suffered at least its second known fire in 1932) prior to Mount Airy's purchase by the current owners, Mr. and Mrs. Frank Kulla. During Mrs. Patterson's period of residence, the plantation once again saw a U.S. president within its walls, for she was a fervent supporter of FDR, and he and his wife were often entertained there.

In 1973, Mount Airy was acquired by the Maryland State Department of Natural Resources and turned into the over-1,000-acre Rosaryville State Park. As a result of inadequate funds, the mansion was allowed to stand vacant and virtually unattended for ten years until it was seen by the Kullas, who wanted to buy Mount Airy and turn it once again into a restaurant. Four years of extensive restoration work have succeeded in reviving the lost charm and grandeur of the historic home, and, some believe, may have given new life as well to some of its ghostly inhabitants.

Rumors of a haunted Mount Airy have circulated for years. In the 1930s, the home was included in Mrs. Marguerite du Pont Lee's book of haunted Maryland and Virginia homes. It also has been visited by a team of investigators from the London Society for Psychical Research. According to one story, the ghost of Elizabeth Bresco Calvert walks the mansion's dark halls at night searching for hidden jewels. Additionally, there are the spirits of a heartbroken young girl in white who has returned to mourn a love forbidden her in life; an old woman who roams from room to room at night, waking sleeping occupants; and a horseman in old-fashioned riding attire. A former owner, Tillie Duvall, tells of having returned home late one night to encounter this latter personage at Mount Airy's entrance. Mrs. Duvall also recalls a particular haunted room where a candle would not stay lit and whose door contantly opened and closed by itself. Another tale surrounds the last member of the Calvert family to live in the mansion, a somewhat eccentric Miss Eleanor Calvert, who died there in 1902 at the age of eighty-one. According to legend, Miss Eleanor did not like to have the front parlor used. After she died as a result of a fall down some stairs, her body was nevertheless laid out in the front parlor the night before the funeral. The next day, the key to the room, whose door had been locked, could not be found. The parlor had to be broken into and the key was discovered within, on a table next to Miss Eleanor's coffin.

The present owners, Frank and Patricia Kulla, regard the stories of their haunted restaurant with a sense of humor. While they're not actually averse to the idea of ghosts, they just can't admit to having seen any themselves. Patricia, however, does admit she gets a certain "feeling" inside the house, but she attributes it to Mount Airy's sense of history and her own fertile imagination.

On the other hand, she does recall several incidents which she still can't fully explain. People involved in restoration of the house have told her some rather odd things. On one occasion, a workman who had arrived at his usual early hour of seven o'clock swore that he saw a man in a red shirt standing at a second-story window. Not only shouldn't there have been anyone inside the house at that time, but there was also no second floor then for the man to stand on. Another time, a superintendent and his foreman were at Mount Airy after dusk one chilly winter evening when they both watched a door open by itself. After they closed the door and watched it slowly open a second time, they abandoned their work in haste. Although they later checked the door and its hinges, they could never determine the cause for the door having opened itself. Following that incident, they both refused to work after sundown.

Of practical mind and bent, Mrs. Kulla takes the ghostly reports in stride and blames many things on overactive imaginations. She recalls one incident, however, that happened to her. Once, she says, she spotted a patch of white light through a window when she was standing outside the house. She knew that there were no lights on in the house and she also realized that it couldn't be a reflection of anything. To this day, Mrs. Kulla remains uncertain of what she saw, but does not let this uncertainty bother her. She and her husband are far too busy with their living guests to worry about the activities of any nonliving ones.

Maidstone's Gray Lady

Probably the most legendary haunted house in Calvert County is Maidstone, home of Mrs. Jean Hicks since 1949. Built in the late seventeenth century by Samuel Chew on a 2,000-acre tract of land, Maidstone was well known from its earliest years since it was used as a Quaker meetinghouse by the Chews. The house remained in the Chew family for almost 200 years. Although the original wood structure rotted away, a second Maidstone was built nearby in the mid-1700s.

Maidstone's reputation for being haunted predates its purchase by the Hicks family. According to accounts given by the Wilsons, the family that owned the house prior to the Hickses, a beautiful young woman dressed in gray was often seen by various people over the years. The description of the woman matches that of an early Chew family member, Ann, who was married to Philip Chew at Maidstone in 1724. Even members of the Chew family are said to have seen Ann's majestic figure quietly walking the grounds of the old homestead. Reportedly, Ann has always been sighted on a moonlit night in the vicinity of Maidstone's gardens and has virtually always been described as being exceedingly graceful and wearing a long, gray veil almost four feet in length. Many people believe that the dress she is seen wearing is her wedding gown, and over the years Ann has acquired the name "The Gray Lady."

The Gray Lady has rarely been sighted within the house itself

although one of the Wilsons is said to have seen her walk out of the house as he was making his way back to it from the stable. The apparition supposedly stopped in her journey long enough to give the man a friendly smile before continuing on her way. Another Wilson gentleman told stories of numerous encounters with the young woman, including some in the house when he used to be rudely awakened by someone pushing him off the couch he was napping on. He also attributed to Ann Chew the unexplained tendency for a number of pictures hanging in one of Maidstone's halls to be routinely shifted about.

Although several members of the Wilson family witnessed the gray-clad ghost wandering around Maidstone's grounds at night, they did not discuss their experiences with the Hickses when the latter purchased the house. It was not long, however, before Mrs. Hicks learned that everyone in the area was very familiar with the stories of the Gray Lady, even if she were not. Mrs. Hicks distinctly recalls the time she and her husband decided to go out one afternoon and left their three children at home in the care of a neighboring farmer's wife. The effect that Maidstone's reputation had on area residents was all too evident when the Hickses returned to their home as dusk was approaching. Seated in the kitchen, they found not only the farmer's wife, but additional babysitters—the woman's two grown sons armed with loaded shotguns. The three explained that they had intended to prepare themselves for whatever Maidstone had to offer as darkness came.

Despite the almost forty years that Mrs. Hicks has lived in her home and kept a careful eye and ear open for sight or sound of a ghost, she has never seen anything at Maidstone of a paranormal nature. Mrs. Hicks is somewhat regretful that she's never seen the Gray Lady, for she says that she certainly has wanted to. She's still hopeful that one day she, too, will have the opportunity of seeing the lovely Ann Chew.

Westminster's Famous Ghosts

Tales of ghosts and haunted houses are so abundant in the town of Westminster in Carroll County that the Westminster Public Library has even organized a ghost tour of the downtown area. Two of the most interesting stops on the tour are the old Opera House on East Main Street and Cockey's Tavern, also on East Main Street.

Over 100 years ago the Opera House served as Carroll County's center of entertainment. According to a local story, a comedian named Marshall Buell from Alabama was entertaining the Opera House audience one night by making political jokes directed against the government. Buell's anti-Union diatribe did little to endear him to his audience, some of whom were staunchly pro-North. Several irate spectators threw rocks at the comedian and it was necessary for the sheriff to intercede and forcibly remove three men from the Opera House. Later that evening, as Buell was preparing to leave for Hagerstown, the seat of Washington County, he was approached by the sheriff, who volunteered to protect him from any troublemakers still intent on doing the Alabaman bodily harm. Buell refused the sheriff's offer and insisted on making the final preparations for his journey alone. Having packed all of his belongings into one heavy trunk, Buell was carrying it down the back stairs of the Opera House to his waiting horse when he was attacked by an unknown party or parties. The comedian was stabbed and left to die in his own blood at the bottom of the Opera House stairs.

Following the murder of the Southern entertainer, local townsfolk reported seeing the headless body of a man standing near the back stairs of the Opera House, gesturing and motioning as though he were telling jokes and stories to an enthralled audience. The belief that Marshall Buell's ghost had returned to the spot where he met his unfortunate death has persisted over the years. Some people still think that the Opera House is occupied by Buell's ghost, although it is now home to the Opera House Printing Company. With the exterior beautifully restored, the Opera House's interior must seem unfamiliar to Buell, for it has been drastically altered to accommodate the printing business. Nevertheless, some employees insist that strange things often occur in the building where Marshall Buell from Alabama spent his last night.

Farther up East Main Street is Cockey's Tavern, which was built in the early 1800s and which continues to operate as a public purveyor of fine food and spirits. The ghost or ghosts in Cockey's Tavern are very active inhabitants, known for boot-stomping, glass-rattling, and picture-moving. One frequenter of the tavern is the suspected ghost of a Civil War soldier whose heavy boots can be heard tramping up and down the tavern's center stairway. This particular ghost is also said to harbor a fondness for other spirits—namely, the liquor available at the tavern's bar. According to what was reportedly witnessed by one of the tavern's former owners, the soldier now and then helps himself to a drink from the bar, as evidenced by the sound of rattling glasses. Moving the pictures that hang on the tavern's walls also seems to be a favorite source of amusement for the ghost, who is believed to use this activity as a way of expressing himself. A story has it that a tired waitress standing near the stairway complained of the lateness of a particularly noisy card party taking place in the tavern. As if to express complete agreement with the waitress's sentiments, one of the four pictures hanging on the stairway wall promptly sailed off its hanger and landed at the feet of the startled woman. A second incident demonstrating the ghost's affinity for moving pictures occurred when a discussion among some guests of the unexplained activities in the tavern's dining room revealed a disbeliever in the supernatural. Supposedly, one of the female participants in the discussion loudly voiced the opinion that there were no such things as ghosts and that she certainly did not believe in them. As if on cue, a picture hanging on the wall over the woman fell off and struck her on the head.

Another time, a waitress setting tables in the dining room discovered a picture of Ulysses Grant, which usually hung on a nearby wall, turned facedown upon a table frequented regularly by a local lawyer and his wife. Later, the waitress was to learn that the lawyer had died the previous night.

A Householdful

Belle and Dan Fangmeyer's
brick house in the Westminster countryside is an unusual one for
several reasons. The first of these is that it was built by Christian
Royer in 1827 as a meetinghouse for the Church of the Brethren
out of Royer's desire to become a church speaker. Not much more
has been discovered of the house's specific history, although it is
known that it was used as both a private residence and a meetinghouse for many years by Royer and his descendants. In more recent
years the house and its surrounding acreage came to be known as
the Leppo Farm. Now it is called Living Faith Farm and Belle
Fangmeyer operates a small antique shop out of it.

The Fangmeyer home is also unusual for the amount of unexplained activity that has occurred in it since Belle, Dan, and their
two teenage daughters, Dana and Nicole, moved into it in December 1985. Belle remembers being immediately struck by an almost
overwhelming feeling of warmth the first time she saw the house,
and still marvels at how so many seemingly impossible obstacles to
their purchase of the property seemed to disappear when she
decided that she really wanted to live there.

During the first month of the Fangmeyers' residence in their
new home, Belle spent many hours alone doing repair and renovation work. She remembers frequently having had the feeling that
there was someone else in the house with her. All of the family

members soon began to notice problems with the stereo set and the VCR. Both appliances would often be found turned on although no one in the family had been using them, and the stereo's radio component would switch stations all by itself in the middle of a transmission. Other, even more obvious incidents shortly followed. A basement door located by the family room would open and close itself, particularly when the family was gathered together relaxing in the family room. The Fangmeyers' pet dog, a terrier, would go to the guest bedroom upstairs and bark for no apparent reason. One day, shortly after Belle had finished painting the ceiling in the living room, she and her husband discovered scribbles on it made with what looked like a brown crayon. The writing appeared to be that of a child. Neither Belle nor Dan could make out the words and both were puzzled by the knowledge that no one in the family could have been responsible for the marks because there were no crayons kept in the house.

Up to this point, Dan still believed that a rational explanation could be found to account for the strange incidents taking place in his home. He thought that it might have been an insect that had caused the brown scribble on the ceiling. His attitude, however, changed somewhat following an encounter he had with one of the house's unseen visitors. Walking up the stairs to the second floor, he thought he heard a disturbance in the master bedroom. As he reached the door, he was startled to see the dog come racing out of the adjoining master bathroom, closely followed by a small wicker wastebasket sailing through the air about five feet off the ground. There was no doubt about it. It looked as though the object had been hurled at the dog. No one, however, was in the bathroom or even in the upstairs part of the house.

Belle guesses that if her home is haunted, then it is being haunted by more than just one ghost, for the varying types of activity seem to point to different personalities behind them. During the family's second Christmas in the house, for instance, they all heard the sound of small feet running up and down the upstairs hall. Also, the family has heard the sound of a child's ball dropping down the steps. Belle feels sure that these noises and the writing on the living room ceiling were the work of a child, rather than an adult. Most recently someone has taken to removing the cushions from the living room furniture and stacking them or putting them on the floor. Objects on a nearby coffee table have been moved sometime during almost every night.

Many relatives and friends, as well as complete strangers, have witnessed the antics of the spirits at Living Faith Farm. During the family's first Thanksgiving in their home, Belle's father complained that the dog under the table had kept tugging at his sports coat while he was seated for dinner. Belle had to reluctantly admit to her father that the dog wasn't in the house and consequently could not have been the thing pulling at his jacket. Several days after the family's second Christmas in their home, guests invited over for a dinner party had the unexpected experience of witnessing one of the more dramatic supernatural events in the Fangmeyers' residence. Standing in several small groups, the people in the dining room watched with widened eyes as a lit candle was taken out of its holder on a nearby table by some invisible hand, carried a distance of about six feet, blown out, and dropped to the floor. Undoubtedly, few of those guests have yet forgotten that dinner party. During still another party, several guests were locked out as they were gathered on a side porch. The door connecting the porch to the house had been inexplicably locked from the inside.

Oftentimes visitors to the antique shop will encounter one of the Fangmeyers' ghosts. An elderly couple swore that they had seen a man dressed in a Civil War uniform sitting in the front porch rocking chair. Upon subsequent research, Belle was able to verify that a member of the Royer family had fought in the war and had been brought back to the house to die after suffering a fatal stomach wound.

Another ghost may have been seen by a family friend who claimed that he saw a woman standing behind Belle the entire evening he had spent visiting her and her husband. Both Belle and her sister-in-law have at various times heard the sound of a man talking and Belle has also heard a woman's voice in the house. She has seen what she believes to have been one of her spirit residents on two different occasions—both times in the area between the living and dining rooms. She describes what she saw as a shapeless form about four feet tall with a brightness to it much like the type you see when a flashbulb goes off in your eyes.

Other manifestations at Living Faith Farm have included the discovery of the words "my love" written on a window screen—again, apparently in a child's hand—and odd behavior often displayed by the two family cats. According to Belle, the cats fight incessantly over the rights to a rocking chair in the family room. Once on it, whichever cat is there will stretch out and purr as though it is being petted. The guest bedroom also appears to be a popular place for ghostly activity. People who go into the room for the first time often remark on the abrupt temperature change they experience upon entering, and the Fangmeyers have not been able to determine why that room always feels chillier than other parts of the house. A photograph taken of the room seems to bear additional evidence of its peculiarities. Although there was no special light or shadow in the room at the time a set of pictures was taken of the window and an antique cradle next to it, there is a strange white shape apparent in one of the photographs. Unfortunately, like the many other unusual happenings at the Fangmeyers', this will probably have to remain a question without an answer.

Patty Cannon's Return

Driving west from Delaware on Route 392 one passes a sign along the road just inside the Maryland state line which reads:

> Patty Cannon's house at Johnson's Crossroads where the noted kidnapping group had headquarters as described in George Alfred Townsend's novel "The Entailed Hat." The house borders on Caroline and Dorchester counties and the state of Delaware.

Some folks believe that Patty Cannon, infamous kidnapper, black marketeer, and murderess, has returned to haunt her old habitat in Reliance, Maryland. Patty Cannon's notorious deeds, which took place over a century and a half ago, are still remembered in Reliance and the surrounding towns, and she has been the subject of several books, most notably George Alfred Townsend's *The Entailed Hat.*

Accounts differ as to exactly where Patty Cannon came from. Some say Canada, some say not, but it is generally agreed that she began her nefarious activities in the early 1800s as leader of a gang organized to kidnap free blacks and slaves and sell them on the black market. Legend has it that she was a large gypsyish-looking woman of enormous strength and ruthless character whom few dared to cross.

Patty Cannon's Return

It is said that the townspeople had known of Patty's illegal activities for some time, as well as the fact that the tavern owned and run by her son-in-law Joe Johnson in Johnson's Crossroads, as Reliance was then called, also served as a holding place for the gang's kidnap victims. Local law enforcers were apparently reluctant to halt Patty's operations, given both the relative lack of concern over the fate of slaves and free blacks at that time as well as the difficulty presented by the state and county borders. Story has it that Patty and her gang eluded arrest on many an occasion by slipping over the state border when authorities from the other state got too close. Consequently, the Patty Cannon gang was able to operate for a number of years out of Reliance, evading law enforcers and rousing among local townspeople only vague suspicions of darker deeds.

In the late 1820s, however, a farmer plowing a cornfield near the tavern unearthed several skeletons, and Patty and her gang were soon linked to a dozen or so murders, including, some say, her own husband's. Patty's career came to an abrupt halt in 1829 when she was arrested and taken to Georgetown, Delaware, to await trial for murder. She was never brought to trial, however, and the exact number of people who died at her hands will never be known, for Patty committed suicide by taking poison reportedly hidden in the hem of her skirt.

Over the years, stories of Patty and her crimes lingered on in the area. It was decided to change the town's name from Johnson's Crossroads to Reliance for propriety's sake, and people talked of the torture and murders supposedly carried out in the attic of the tavern where the Cannon gang's kidnap victims were kept in chains before sale. Nevertheless, despite these grisly tales, both the tavern and Patty's house, located about 200 yards from the tavern, knew many occupants as time went on.

Joe Johnson's tavern still stands today, although much remodeled, with the sign at its side noting its historical significance. The tavern's current owners are Mr. and Mrs. Jack Messick, who purchased it in January 1982. Jack, a retired Marine Corps colonel, teaches elementary school, while his wife Rose is kept busy at home with the youngest of their four sons, Chris, eleven, and Jason, eight. A great deal of work has been done on the large, two-story house, both inside and out, and there is nothing unusual about it from all appearances.

Prior to the Messicks' ownership of the old tavern, however, stories of Patty Cannon and her gang resurfaced and it was rumored among the locals that Patty's ghost had returned when the then owner of the tavern began experiencing strange things. He apparently became convinced that he was not living alone. Eerie noises and sounds of footsteps, doors slamming shut, and the sensation of an evil presence in certain parts of the house all contributed to strengthening the owner's conviction that Patty and her victims had returned to the site where so many were purported to have met their tragic end at her hands. At that time, the house was a museum open to the public for a small admission price, and people were led through the tavern, where they could see the attic "dungeon," alleged scene of so many crimes. That all ended when the owner vacated the house, claiming, it was said, that he couldn't bear to live amidst its ghostly goings-on anymore.

Although some local people still believe the tavern to be haunted, the Messick family has not experienced anything more unearthly than unexpected visitors dropping by at odd times in search of ghosts or buried treasure (another story has it that gold is buried in the cornfield behind the tavern). The house is attractively decorated in colonial style and it shows the signs of being inhabited only by a happy, active family. The trapdoor up to the attic is in the master bedroom, but the Messicks do not use the attic and do not seem at all bothered by the attic's infamous past.

Has Patty Cannon returned to the site of her crimes? Well, stories die hard and certainly the legends of her deeds lend easy fuel to the fires of one's imagination. My guess is that the ghosts, if any, probably abandoned all hope of outdoing the shenanigans of two fun-loving young boys and decided to take their frightening bag of tricks elsewhere.

PATTY CANNON'S HOUSE
AT JOHNSON'S CROSS ROADS WHERE
THE NOTED KIDNAPPING GROUP HAD
HEADQUARTERS AS DESCRIBED IN
GEORGE ALFRED TOWNSEND'S NOVEL
"THE ENTAILED HAT". THE HOUSE
BORDERS ON CAROLINE AND DOR-
CHESTER COUNTIES AND THE STATE
OF DELAWARE.

The Unexplained Smell

Mr. Abel (not his real name) can still remember that terrible smell. It was the smell of human excrement and it permeated the interior of the house. It was embarrassing and at times so powerful that it made breathing difficult. It was just one of the things that finally led him to sell the house that had been in the family since 1898.

The house that Mr. Abel sold two years ago still stands and it is not known whether the current owner has experienced any of the same phenomena that the Abel family can even today so vividly recall. Located in Brunswick, a small town of about 4,500 people in southern Frederick County, the two-story wood frame house has been extensively remodeled. When Mr. Abel's grandfather moved into the house in 1898, there was no known tragedy or unusual event associated with it. As the years passed, however, all of the members of the Abel family grew to realize that something peculiar was associated with their home.

Mr. Abel remembers that things began to happen with intensity when he reached the age of sixteen. He and his younger sister were the only children in the house in the 1940s. By that time, both of his grandparents had passed away and the house now belonged to his father. First, there was a pecking sound that could be heard throughout the house. No explanation for the persistent noise was ever found. Then family members began to notice an odor of chrysanthemums that would come and go, without any known cause. Small beads of water would develop on the first-floor ceiling, although no reason for the moisture could be determined.

Later, things became more frightening. The family began to notice a different smell, one of a much less pleasant nature. It was so strong that they worried about having company over. The sounds of footsteps on the stairs to the second floor could be heard and it often seemed as though there were someone moving around in the upstairs bedrooms. At other times, doors would slam shut by themselves or an eerie silence would fall heavily over the house and its occupants. Once, Mr. Abel's mother walked into the living room and saw the rocking chair there rocking by itself. Another time, both his parents heard a tremendous thump from one of the upstairs bedrooms. Realizing that neither of the children could have been responsible for the noise since they hadn't been upstairs, Mr. Abel's father searched all three bedrooms without finding a clue to the noise.

Unnatural activity in the house became so intense that the family decided to hold a séance in the living room one afternoon in order to communicate with whatever was causing all of the trouble. Once seated in the semidarkened living room, the family gave instructions for the unseen entity to communicate with them by knocking. One knock would signify "yes," two knocks "no." According to Mr. Abel, things "got out of hand" very quickly after that. A loud pounding began to sound on the floor. When the family realized that none of them was making the noise, they became frightened and broke off the séance.

Since many of the noises seemed to come from the cellar, it was investigated for some sort of explanation. Although he searched the dirt-floor basement thoroughly, Mr. Abel's father could not find anything to account for the disturbances.

Thirty-five years passed after these incidents occurred and Mr. Abel grew up and moved out to raise a family of his own. In 1979, he decided to assume ownership of the family home and moved back to it with his wife and three sons. They were in the house for one year before things began to happen. It was almost as if history were repeating itself. The noises once again began to resound throughout the house and the terrible stench of excrement returned. This did not encourage Mr. Abel and his family to remain. In view of the fact that his wife never appreciated the house's eccentricities, Mr. Abel decided that the time had come to sell the house, even if it did mean giving up what had been a family residence for generation after generation. To this day, Mr. Abel does not regret his decision. He remembers only too well the disturbing occurrences that affected his and his family's lives for years.

The Nanny Ghost

Time seems to have changed little in Smithsburg, a small town in Washington County. Its farms and fields are often enshrouded in a low-lying fog which parts at times along the rugged terrain of crags and rocks to reveal old country farmhouses. Doug and Teresa Bachtell's pre-Civil War home is one of these often mist-enveloped houses. Although it has been carefully restored to eradicate the ravages of time, both time and history have left their imprint on the Bachtell residence.

The first sign the Bachtells had that there was something unusual about their new home occurred just prior to their moving into it eight years ago. According to Teresa, her mother and sister had volunteered to help clean the house about a week before the Christmas holidays. The two women were alone in the house when they both heard the intermittent chiming of a grandfather's clock. Unable to find any such item in the house, the women concluded that the odd noise had probably issued from a clock that Doug had, they thought, purchased for Teresa as a Christmas present. Upon questioning, however, Doug said that he hadn't bought one. No explanation could be found for the mysterious chiming.

After the Bachtells had moved into their home with their two young sons, Chip and Colby, other odd things happened. Lights would go on and off by themselves, the television and electric fans would likewise function for no apparent reason, and the chimes of the invisible grandfather's clock were heard once again.

It was not until Teresa had her third son, Patrick, several months after the move, that more than just small oddities became commonplace. For some reason, whenever Doug or Teresa went to check on Patrick in his crib, they would invariably find his covers perfectly tucked in around him and his pacifier neatly in place in his mouth. As if that weren't strange enough, Patrick was rarely, if ever, known to cry when he was put in his crib, no matter how long he was left there. In fact, he always seemed very content to be left in his crib, and his mother often got the eerie impression that he was being entertained by someone or something in his room.

Although Teresa had seen the rocking chair in her son's room move back and forth by itself, neither she nor her husband held more than just a vague suspicion of a possible ghostly guest until one night when they were returning home from a Christmas party. The three Bachtell boys had been left with Doug's seventeen-year-old sister Cindy while Teresa and Doug went out for the evening. Feeling slightly uneasy over having left Patrick while he was cutting teeth, Teresa's misgivings increased when the car pulled into the driveway and she glanced out of the car window to the house. Silhouetted in the bathroom window on the second floor, Cindy was standing with Patrick in her arms, patting him on the back. Evidently, the baby had been crying and giving her a hard time. Teresa immediately got out of the car and hurried to the front door. As she passed through the family room, she noticed Cindy soundly asleep on the couch. As Teresa says, "I didn't even stop, but just kept right on going to Patrick's room." She climbed the stairs to her son's room and, reaching it, paused. Nothing seemed amiss. Patrick was lying in his crib, awake, a small smile on his face and his blankets all in place. Later, when questioned as to whether the baby had been crying that evening, Cindy told her brother and sister-in-law that the baby had given her no trouble at all. She'd put him to bed at eight that evening and hadn't heard a peep out of him. Clearly, she had not been the one who had picked Patrick up to calm his crying.

As time passed, the Bachtells became more and more convinced that their son had someone who looked after him, and family members became used to the idea of an additional household member, even referring to it as Patrick's "nanny ghost." Not everything, however, could be explained by Patrick's ghostly nursemaid.

On one occasion a friend of Teresa's from Silver Spring, Maryland, who had planned to spend the night with the Bachtells, reconsidered her decision after having had her sleep disturbed by a small blonde-haired girl. The friend told her hosts that the girl, dressed in an old-fashioned white nightgown, kept trying to climb into bed with her. Clearly disturbed by the incident, the woman decided to return to her own home that very night.

An unrelated, albeit still unsettling, event that Teresa experienced seemed to reach far back into the house's history. One day, while recovering from an illness, she witnessed a dreamlike scene unfolding before her. Teresa recalls seeing shapes start to form in the corner of the room. As they grew more distinct, she was able to make out the figures of several male slaves huddled around an early type of stove. They were dressed alike in old-fashioned, large-sleeved white shirts, of the kind worn in the midnineteenth century, and were discussing moving someone out to the underground railroad. Teresa remembers that they kept gesturing out the window toward the north. As unexpectedly as the vision had appeared, it faded, and Teresa was left to contemplate the significance of what she had seen. With little personal knowledge of American Civil War history and not much desire to acquire more, Teresa realized that the vision had not been produced by her overactive imagination. She just didn't know enough to have been able to even attribute the correct period costumes to the group of men she had seen in her room talking about escape to the North. Later, when she researched the history of the house, Teresa was able to determine that it had indeed been part of the underground railroad system.

The Bachtells were careful to keep the stories about their home's strange occupants in the family for fear of ridicule. In 1982, however, the story leaked out, and several of the ghostly incidents were reported in a local newspaper in connection with Halloween.

Ghosts & Haunted Houses of Maryland

Shortly after the story's publication, Teresa received a phone call from an elderly woman in a nursing home who introduced herself as Mrs. Bope. She told Teresa that she had read the newspaper account of the Bachtells' house and believed that she could provide an explanation. According to the elderly woman, her daughter and blonde-haired granddaughter had lived in the house in the 1930s. The granddaughter, Molly, had become ill and died of kidney failure in the house when she was not yet three years old. She had been buried in a white nightgown handmade by her grandmother. Mrs. Bope's daughter had been inconsolable after the death of Molly and had begun to pretend that her other young child, a boy, was the daughter she had lost. She became hopelessly insane and was institutionalized until her death.

Mrs. Bope told Teresa that she was certain that her daughter had returned to her old home and that it was she who had become Patrick's nanny ghost. The young girl in a white nightgown who had been seen by Teresa's friend was probably Molly.

Interviewed about four years after she received the phone call from Mrs. Bope, Teresa says that unusual things continue to happen occasionally in the house but the odd occurrences seemed to subside drastically following an encounter she believes she had with her son's nanny ghost. She remembers that it had been a particularly dreadful day for her because she had been sick and had been caring both for Patrick and his new sister Rachel. Patrick had been put in his crib but kept crying because he wanted "the lady" to go away. Exhausted after having climbed the stairs countless times to calm her son in his bedroom, Teresa decided that enough was enough. She went into Patrick's room and directed her attention to the still-moving rocking chair in the corner. She addressed its invisible occupant and explained that while she had appreciated its help in the past, Patrick was old enough to realize that a nanny ghost was not necessarily a normal part of every boy's life. He had become scared of the ghost and now he needed to be left alone. And leave the nanny ghost has, for the most part. Only rarely now does Teresa feel the woman's presence in her home.

The Ghost in the Picture

Leitersburg is a small, sleepy town in northern Washington County not far from the Pennsylvania border. Named for James Van Leiter, a Dutch Calvinist who came to Baltimore in the 1760s, Leitersburg is home to more than a few historic buildings. Pete and Jeanine Humphrey's house on Main Street may well be the most historic dwelling in town. The large gray brick structure was built by a member of the Leiter family circa 1850 and the Humphreys suspect that it may be a Leiter who has chosen to stay on in the house.

It wasn't long after Pete and Jeanine moved into the house about twelve years ago that they both began to notice some persistent noises emanating from the basement, or so it seemed. Being levelheaded sorts, neither Pete nor his wife paid much attention to the sounds, attributing them to the normal noises made by an old house. A loud, rather hollow-sounding thump would often be heard two or three times in succession and then would stop. Footsteps could be heard on the stairs to the second floor and in the upstairs bedrooms. Lights would go on and off by themselves. Added to these oddities was the uncanny feeling both the Humphreys had of never really being alone in the house even when they thought they were. They began to conclude that all was not what it seemed.

It wasn't until several incidents of somewhat greater significance occurred, however, that the Humphreys' vague suspicions grew into a strong feeling that they were not living alone. As Mr. Humphrey relates, a young neighborhood boy was over visiting one day when the noises in the basement began their usual routine. Intent on locating their source, Pete asked his eight-year-old guest if he'd like to go down to the basement "to catch the ghost." The boy agreed and the two stationed themselves at different areas in the basement. After several minutes, each became convinced that the noise was coming from the area where the other was standing. Upon meeting at a central point and continuing to hear the noise, Mr. Humphrey and the boy decided to abandon their quest. It had been impossible to track down the source of the sounds.

A subsequent event which considerably increased the Humphreys' misgivings involved an old pump in the cellar that had been used years before to pump cistern water into the house. Shortly after moving in, Pete had determined that the pump's electric motor was virtually inoperable, and had disconnected it by removing the two fuses to its wires. The fuses were carefully placed on top of the fuse box and no further thought was given to the matter.

Some time later, Mrs. Humphrey returned from a morning spent shopping only to be confronted by the smell of smoke when she walked into the house. The smoke seemed to be coming from downstairs, so she opened the door to the basement. Smoke poured out and Jeanine heard a cacophony that sounded like the old pump. She quickly turned off all power to the house and was relieved to be unable to find any fire. Later, when Mr. Humphrey investigated, he found that the pump had been turned on and operated with such intensity that its fanbelt had burnt through. The two fuses, however, had not been touched and still sat in the thick layer of dust that had settled over them from disuse. Neither Pete, an electrical engineer, nor Jeanine could ever discover how the pump had been turned on or by whom.

Pete Humphrey's 1928 Model A Ford is the apple of his eye and he has spent years restoring it to its former splendor. He has guarded its welfare carefully, keeping it in the basement garage

during the winter and watching over it with a keen eye. Great was his dismay one afternoon when, after having decided to take the car out for a drive, Pete discovered that its meter was showing an electrical discharge, indicating that the car's generator probably needed replacement. Pete took the car over to a friend who was also involved in antique car restoration and both men examined it. The car's instrument panel was removed and the culprit soon found. Although the Model A's factory wiring had never been replaced, somehow the two wires connecting the meter and the generator had been crossed. Mr. Humphrey had not touched the wires and no one had had access to the garage where the car was kept. Crossing the wires had been no simple achievement—the car's instrument panel would have had to be removed for the wires to have been rearranged.

Both Humphreys have a relaxed attitude about the goings-on at their house and have even jokingly blamed the mischief on the ghost of Levi Leiter, a famous merchant of the nineteenth century who amassed a fortune through his business ventures. Leiter, who died in 1904, was particularly instrumental in aiding Chicago's recovery after its devastation in the infamous 1871 fire.

That the Humphreys' invisible ghost is Levi Leiter may very well be true. A color snapshot Pete took of his car parked alongside the curb outside the front of the house adds an interesting note to this story. Pete liked to take pictures of his car during various stages of its restoration and would accordingly park it in the street and take a picture of it without any occupants. Apparently, however, someone has taken a shine to Pete's old car, for when he had a set of photos developed, one clearly shows a man seated in the front— although the car was empty when the picture was taken. The car's occupant is a middle-aged gentleman with long whiskers, dressed in clothes of the type prevalent in this area of Maryland in the late nineteenth century—a broad-brimmed hat atop his head, a white shirt, black trousers, and suspenders. He is clearly a person, and not a shadow of nearby trees or other objects. I know, for I have seen the picture.

The Noises at Cedar Hill

Cedar Hill in Calvert County near Barstow is the only example of cruciform domestic architecture now standing in southern Maryland. The brick one-and-a-half-story house, center of a tobacco plantation, was built in the early 1700s on 5,000 acres of land deeded in 1666. It was the second-largest homesite in the county. Cedar Hill's imaginative builder is thought to have been John Bigger, whose name was found on an eighteenth-century deed. The builder, whoever he may have been, was apparently something of an engineer and astronomer, for he purposely constructed the house in the shape of a cross. Intriguingly, the cross is positioned so that twice a year, during the spring and fall equinoxes, the sun passes directly over the long axis of the building, from the front door to the back of the house. Consequently six months of the year the sun rises and sets on the north side of the house, and the other six months of the year on the south side. (Several additions have been made to the original structure, the most recent one in 1938.) Cedar Hill is also unusual in that it is one of the few old homes that appears to have been constantly occupied.

Twenty years ago, Eric Schneider first saw Cedar Hill and decided to buy it and rent it out until he was able to live in it himself. The first stories of strange happenings at Cedar Hill began with some of Eric's tenants. One woman used to complain that a throw rug she used in a downstairs hallway was always being rolled up and pushed to one side of the hall no matter how many times she straightened it out.

Harry and Lenore Markard's unexplained experiences in the home in the early 1980s began the day they and their children moved in, when a door inexplicably slammed shut behind Harry's brother, who was helping with the move. The television set and several light switches would turn on by themselves and one of Lenore's sisters was once mysteriously tapped on the shoulder by an unseen hand while visiting at the house. Yet another time, Harry and his nephew were carrying wood through the kitchen when a door slammed shut by itself behind them. The same nephew thought that he saw a man dressed in a Civil War uniform standing in the den one night.

The most disturbing incident that happened to the Markards during their year-and-a-half stay at Cedar Hill involved Harry. For some time, the family had heard odd noises coming from the attic area. Harry decided to investigate; after searching the attic without having been able to locate anything, he turned to come back down the attic stairs. Suddenly, he felt something from behind push him and he fell the length of the stairway. Fortunately, he was not seriously injured, although he still carries a scar where a nail on the side of the stairway caught his arm on the way down. No one was ever able to find out the reason for the seemingly unprovoked attack.

The ghost, however, is not without some sense of humor. On one occasion, Harry was trying to pull the basement door shut but was unable to, as it kept being pulled by someone or something on the other side. After this tug-of-war scene had gone on for several minutes, Harry decided to give up. He shrugged his shoulders and said, "Okay, I don't care." Immediately, the door swung shut.

According to Harry and Lenore, the supernatural activities at Cedar Hill came to an end after they decided to clean up an area they had found near the house that contained the graves of some much earlier residents. Weeding and minor adjustments to fallen gravestones seemed to appease Cedar Hill's unseen presence and the Markards, at least, were no longer troubled by strange events in their home.

The unexplained noises and activities at the old house were not to be stopped for long, however. Shortly after Eric and his wife Carol took up permanent residence at Cedar Hill, they began to hear the sound of a rocking chair rocking back and forth. The sound seems to come from the attic, and both day and night is highly audible in the master bedroom directly below it. Eric says that many nights the sound continues for hours—sometimes, he suspects, long after he and Carol have fallen off to sleep. Eric has not been able to find any explanation for the rocking chair noise although, like Harry, he has searched the attic thoroughly. Maybe it is time for the old graveyard to be tidied up again.

Laurel's
Most Haunted House

At last count, there were five ghosts at the old Georgian mansion called Oaklands, which was built from ballast bricks in the 1700s by Richard Snowden. Located on forty acres in the town of Laurel in northern Prince George's County, the house once stood on thousands of acres. Snowden built it for his daughter as a wedding gift and over time it passed into the hands of other families.

In the 1920s Oaklands was purchased by Mr. Staggart, the grandfather of Pam Pecor Unger and John Pecor, both of whom now live on the property with their spouses. Pam remembers having first heard stories of the old mansion's ghosts from her grandmother, who claimed that some people had seen the spirit of Richard Contee, one of the home's earlier owners, on Oaklands' grounds. When Pam was a teenager, her family came to live in the house and she began to notice strange things about it as soon as they moved in. Between nine and ten o'clock each night, the young girl would distinctly hear from her bedroom the sounds of a horse galloping up the driveway, the front door of the house opening and closing as if someone were entering, and footsteps in the hallway. The sounds would then occur in reverse after a brief period, until Pam heard the sound of the horse's hooves galloping away. Often, she would notice that a perfumelike smell of apple blossoms permeated her room and she could sometimes hear the sound of a rocking chair rocking back and forth in the third-floor bedroom above hers.

It was also in her bedroom that she had her first glimpse of the ghost of a young child. Having just finished reading in bed before turning off her bed light and going to sleep, Pam suddenly noticed that a little boy of about five was seated on the edge of her bed. The boy was close enough for Pam to see his blue eyes and notice that he was dressed in old-fashioned clothes—a light brown suit with shorts and a rounded shirt collar. Unalarmed, she watched him and waited for him to go away, but found that he was just as intent on watching her watching him. Finally, Pam recalls, she decided to turn off her light and go to sleep. She has since seen the same boy three or four other times in the house and believes that he might be the ghost of one of the Contee family's many children. John Pecor and a blacksmith once employed by the family have also seen the boy.

In addition to the child, several people, including Pam's mother, have seen the ghost of a large black woman. Pam herself has seen the apparition of a black man dressed in the work clothes of a much earlier era. Noting that Oaklands was once a working farm with over 200 slaves, Pam feels that these two individuals might have once worked at the mansion.

John Pecor has a ghost story that will rival most in its unusualness. About seven years ago John was outside the house when he noticed a very attractive young woman in a long dress beckoning to him from across the front lawn. Mystified, he followed her and eventually was led to an area near one of the terraces. The strange woman stopped and, pointing down toward the grass at her feet, disappeared. When John looked at the place she had indicated, he found a gold jewelry chain. He later took the chain to a local jeweler who identified its material and workmanship as those of the eighteenth century. John, who has seen the woman again within the past year, believes, as does his sister, that the woman had been concerned with trying to clear herself of some past misdeed connected with the chain. Consequently, she had been determined to show someone where the jewelry was.

Other supernatural phenomena at the mansion have been of a more frightening nature. While sleeping in the master bedroom, Pam's husband, Bill Unger, was awakened by the sound of heavy, dragging footsteps. Sensing rather than seeing something, Bill could hear the sound of someone's breathing drawing closer to him until the presence actually was bending over him. Unable to move or shout, he lay immobilized for an indefinite period of time while the terrifying thing stubbornly maintained its position. At last, Bill was able to poke Pam, who was sleeping next to him, into wakefulness. As soon as she awoke, the presence was gone.

Oaklands has had other not-so-pleasant happenings. Both John and Pam have heard the sound of a woman crying somewhere in the house. Several people have heard a terrible scream coming from a wooded area on Oaklands' grounds. The same woods were the scene of a murder over fifty years ago when a local Laurel woman was killed there. Her assailant was never found. Other times, Oaklands' residents just have the strange sensation of being watched. One evening Bill was out near the stables when he swore that someone was following him as he walked on a path in the area.

The Ungers and Pecors have learned to live with their ghostly visitors gracefully, however, and Pam has even succeeded in putting an end to one particularly annoying ghostly habit. Irritated that someone seemed to take great pleasure in interrupting her activities whenever she was preparing to take a bath or shower by ringing an old farm bell outside the house and making her go down to see who it was, Pam took down the farm bell. Now she's satisfied that she has some control over at least a few of her home's ghostly happenings.

The Friendly Ghost

Also in Laurel, just over the line in Howard County, is Linda and John Armstrong's wood frame Victorian style farmhouse. The house is at least 100 years old and was once part of a working farm. Linda hasn't been able to find out much about her home's early owners, but the previous owner had lived there for the last forty years.

When the Armstrongs bought the house in 1979 it needed extensive restoration work, which they carried out with a great eye for detail. To step into their home is to step back a hundred years in time, for even the furniture is antique. Several years after purchasing the house, a beauty shop that Linda runs was added to the original structure, neatly incorporating the old and the new.

Linda says it was not long after she and her family had moved in that she began to be aware of noises occurring at different times in the house when no one was in the area to be causing them. Although the Armstrongs have two cats, the cats spend most of their time outdoors. At the times the noises were heard in the house, both of the pets were known to be outside. Most of the sounds seemed to originate from two different areas of the house: the kitchen and a small upstairs bedroom used for storage. Linda remembers being aware of sounds like boxes being dropped and moved around in both locations and then blaming the noise on her teenage son who always denied having made it. Once, Linda was home late at night seated in her living room reading when she began to hear the now-usual noises in the kitchen, which is situated toward the back of the house. The disturbance continued and Linda grew steadily more nervous until she was startled by the unexpected appearance of one of the cats nonchalantly sauntering into the living room from the hallway. Linda knew that both of the cats had been put outside and that there was no way for them to get back into the house unless someone let them in—the same someone responsible for the noises in the kitchen. Convinced that there was a prowler in her home, she quietly and quickly crossed the hallway to the master bedroom to call the police from the phone there. Arriving a short time later, the police searched both the house and the grounds but were unable to find any evidence of an intruder.

For several years afterward, the activity at the Armstrongs' was less overt. Linda describes often having had a feeling of someone watching her when she knew that she was alone in the house, or having seen vague shapes flit past the corner of her eye to disappear when she turned to follow them. Within the past year, however, both she and her husband witnessed a very overt demonstration of their home's unseen presence when they were awakened in the middle of the night by an unexpected visitor.

John was the first to see the white-gowned woman with long, dark hair who stood at the foot of their bed, gazing down at them. After several minutes, Linda awoke and saw the figure. Neither of them said anything to the other, and after a short while both fell back asleep. The next day, Linda remembers her husband telling her that he had had the oddest dream. When he described it to her, they both realized that it hadn't been a dream at all, for they had both seen the same thing.

Several months later, a friend of Linda's father who was visiting the Armstrongs told them that she sensed a "friendly presence" in the house. The woman, who was familiar with automatic handwriting, offered to see if she could make contact with whatever was in their home. After a short session with paper and pen, she produced several pages of legible handwriting which indicated that there was a ghost at the Armstrongs'. According to the messages scrawled on the notepaper, there was a friendly spirit who was residing with the family and who was pleased with all the work they had put into restoring the house.

Noises in the kitchen and in the small bedroom continue, but Linda is the first to admit that now she just takes her home's various unexplained sounds in stride. So far, the friendly ghost has not visited the beauty shop, probably to the great relief of Linda and some of her customers.

The Ghost of Furnace Hills

Reminders of one of Carroll County's most infamous citizens, Legh Master, can be seen in fields everywhere. Master, whose body lies buried in the Ascension Church graveyard in Westminster, is said to have unwittingly introduced the daisy or "Legh Master's clover," as it has come to be called, in the United States by ordering seeds from England that he thought were English clover and planting them. An even less charming reminder of Master is his anguished spirit which is said to haunt his old home of Avondale and the surrounding woods a few miles west of downtown Westminster. Since Master's death in 1796, local townspeople have expressed varying levels of reluctance over venturing into the Avondale area after sunset for fear of seeing his ghost.

Legh Master, or "The Ghost of Furnace Hills," came to what is now Carroll County in the early 1700s and began a smelting business. Known as a slave driver in the most literal sense, Master was so cruel to his slaves that stories of his viciousness soon spread throughout the area. Some people believed that he was responsible for the sudden and unexplained disappearance of Sam, one of his slaves. Rumor had it that Legh did not like Sam, and murdered him by throwing him into one of the smelting furnaces. Master himself lived to the ripe old age of seventy-nine without revealing any knowledge of Sam's whereabouts or confessing to any of the horrific deeds he was suspected of.

Soon after Master's death, stories sprang up of sightings of his ghost astride a wild galloping horse whose nostrils exhaled fire. Master was also seen wandering through the woods near his old home, supposedly regretful of his evil actions on earth and begging for mercy on his soul.

Over the years, Avondale was left to decay, inhabited primarily by tenant farmers who worked the surrounding farmland. In the 1930s, a discovery was made that seemed to support the rumors of Master's evilness—two skeletons were uncovered behind the bricks in a fireplace at Avondale. The skeletons were those of a woman and a child whose identities were never determined. It was rumored that they belonged to Sam's wife and her child by Master. Both were said to have been murdered by Master.

Avondale is presently owned by Helen and Michael Hecht, who purchased the property in 1981 after it had been extensively renovated. No signs of neglect are now visible in the old Master homestead, and, according to the Hechts, neither are any signs of a ghost. Helen, who comes from the area and grew up with a well-versed knowledge of Legh Master's reputation, admits to at first having been reluctant to move into a house with such terrible stories connected with it. Nevertheless, her husband was immediately taken with the place and they decided to buy Avondale with the thought of preserving as much of it and the surrounding land as possible. The Hechts raise cattle and their own food and have little time for the antics of spirits, although they still tell what they regard as the humorous story of a previous Avondale resident who had trouble keeping an upstairs door shut—even after it had been nailed closed. For the Hechts, however, the troublesome door stays shut.

Mary Stewart
of White House Farm

When Mr. and Mrs. Arthur Pinder first bought their dream house in the 1940s, White House Farm near Chestertown in Kent County, they were told about its ghost by the previous owners. According to the story, a young girl named Mary Stewart, who lived there with her family in the early 1800s, decided to elope late one cold January night. Unfortunately, before Mary had even left the property on her way to meet her lover, the horse she was riding bucked and she was thrown to the ground and killed when her head hit a large stone. Local legend has it that Mary has haunted White House Farm and its land ever since. The stone, still on the property today, has reportedly retained the bloodstains left from Mary's fall despite many whitewashings administered by Mr. Pinder. Even the late Mr. Pinder, a staunch nonbeliever in ghosts, could not explain why the stain could not be covered by paint.

White House Farm, a brick structure with white stucco covering it, was built in 1721. When the Pinders bought the house it was sorely in need of restoration and repair, having been rented for some time by a number of different tenant farmers. The Pinders labored for two years to make their new home livable before they moved in. During this time they began to experience some of the unexplained phenomena that the previous owners had told them about. Mrs. Pinder, who, like her husband, is not a believer in ghosts, nevertheless admits to having witnessed many odd things in her home almost immediately after its purchase. Painting in the kitchen one night, both Pinders were startled when they suddenly heard footsteps above them on the second floor. The sound seemed to be made by someone walking from one end of the upstairs to the other. The couple looked at each other in puzzlement but went back to their work when the footsteps stopped a minute later. Soon the sound repeated itself. Wordlessly, the Pinders decided to abandon their painting for the night and return the next day when it was light. They left the house as quickly as they could, not even bothering to put away their work materials. When they returned the following morning, they could find nothing to account for what both knew they had heard.

Mysterious footsteps continued to resound in the Pinder home after the restoration work had been finished and White House Farm was occupied. One evening Mr. Pinder was alone in the kitchen with his two French poodles when he heard strange noises, including footsteps, in the adjacent dining room. It sounded as though someone had just walked into the room from the outside. The two dogs got up and went toward the dining room, stopping at the doorway, their hackles standing straight up. Both animals were growling as though witnessing an intruder making his way into the house. Then Mr. Pinder heard the sound of retreating footsteps and a door opening and closing. The dogs were barking and Mr. Pinder went to the dining room to see what had been the source of the noises. There was no one in the room, and a search outside the house also failed to turn up any evidence of an intruder.

Over the years, the Pinder family grew accustomed to unusual occurrences in their home and they jokingly blamed the things they couldn't explain on the ghost of Mary Stewart. Mrs. Pinder, nonbeliever that she is, thinks that she might have even caught a glimpse of Mary one night when she woke to see a blue-nightgowned figure pass through her bedroom. Thinking that it had been her daughter, she went to the girl's room to find out if anything was wrong. When she questioned her, however, her daughter firmly denied that she had gotten out of bed. She also swore to her mother that she didn't even own a blue nightgown.

Despite their disbelief in the supernatural, the Pinders for years celebrated the anniversary of Mary Stewart's fatal ride by inviting guests to White House Farm every year on the evening of January 8. Local legend said that at midnight on that date Mary Stewart would "walk again." Each year the Pinders and their guests would gather out at the stone where Mary had met her untimely death to await her return. Although no one ever actually saw anything, Mrs. Pinder remembers that there were often strange noises near the stone—noises which she attributes to the hooting of a nearby owl rather than the ghost of Mary Stewart. Perhaps the January evenings were too cold for even a ghost to put in an outdoor appearance.

Two Great (and Haunted)
Houses

Cross the Bay Bridge to the Eastern Shore and you soon enter Talbot County, home of some of the most magnificent old houses in Maryland. Two of these, Gross' Coate and Fairview, are situated close to Easton, the county seat, and both of them have reputations for being haunted as well as beautiful.

The replica of an English country house, Gross' Coate is one of the oldest estates in Maryland, and a stroll up the gravel lane leading to the house will take you years back in history with each advancing step. The 250-year-old home is a world unto itself on its luxurious 63 acres. Although Gross' Coate has been added to over the past 150 years and it has most recently undergone extensive renovation by its current owners, Mr. and Mrs. Jonathan Ginn, a visit to the estate is enough to make the years melt away.

Gross' Coate is the ancestral dwelling of a well-known Talbot family, the Tilghmans, who owned it from its construction circa 1760 until 1983, when it was sold to the Ginns. The most popular ghost story linked to the house involves one of the Tilghmans, "Aunt Molly," who made her home there in the late eighteenth and early nineteenth centuries. Young Mary, or Molly, as she was called, lived with her brother Richard, his wife, and their children in the fateful year of 1790 when she first met the man who would be the love of her life. Charles Willson Peale, the famous portrait painter, had been hired by Richard to paint several members of the family, including Molly. A story has it that Peale, a widower in his forties with several children, became so enamored of the young girl that he asked for her hand in marriage. Although Molly was more than agreeable to Peale's proposal, her sentiments were not shared by her brother. Furious that a man so much older and from a much lower social class should even dare consider marriage to his sister, Richard summarily locked Molly in her room until Peale finished his job and was sent packing.

It is widely believed that the unhappy marriage that Molly did enter into some time later was in retaliation for her brother's earlier interference. According to all accounts, Molly's life after the death of her husband was spent lavishing affection on a favorite nephew, who also had a somewhat rebellious streak. Nights when the nephew would stay out late, Molly would wait upstairs for the sound of his approach and then make her way downstairs where she would unlock the door and let him in.

Over a century after her death, Aunt Molly continues to perform her nightly duties. Generations of Tilghman family members have claimed to have heard the soft tapping of her cane as she walks from room to room, waiting patiently for the return of her nephew. Some people have reportedly even caught a glimpse of her descending the stairs to the first floor to unlock the door. Perhaps, however, Aunt Molly finally tired of her task, for no Ginn family member has seen or heard anything in connection with a ghost. Maybe, like many another elderly aunt, Molly decided that it was high time that her nephew began to look out for himself.

Fairview, also a short drive from Easton, is a lovely home and has been included in the annual Maryland House and Garden Pilgrimage. This handsome yellow brick mansion was built in 1718 on a land grant originally bestowed by Lord Baltimore on Andrew Skinner in 1663. Considered one of the smaller county estates according to a census taken in the late 1700s, Fairview nevertheless boasts one of the most magnificent boxwood gardens in Maryland. The garden, however, has been remembered for many years for

more than just its boxwood—it is the site of strange "voices" from an unknown source that have been heard by visitors to the garden. No one has ever been able to ascertain the cause for the peculiar voices, but you may rest assured that few who know about them venture out to the garden after sundown.

Another favorite haunt of Fairview ghosts is a stretch of land where the gently sloping lawn meets the shore of the Miles River. Here is said to prowl the ghost of a headless man, a British sympathizer still waiting on the beach to guide British vessels to an attack on nearby St. Michaels during the Revolutionary War. On a lane not far from the beach another ghost has been seen astride a magnificent ghost horse madly galloping along the winding road and narrowly missing trees and branches. More than a few visitors have been roused from a peaceful reverie by the wildly racing horseman.

Still other ghosts are said to haunt the old mansion itself. One spirit may be that of the lovely Alicia Lloyd, a member of the famous Lloyd family of Talbot County, who was regarded as a great beauty in her time. Alicia is buried in the family cemetery on the grounds of Fairview and her ghost has been seen passing through doorways and along corridors in a swirl of skirts and petticoats.

Fairview's oldest resident ghost is that of an elderly lady, attired in gray and often found in her favorite spot by the fireplace in the drawing room. Even Mrs. Doris Rend, Fairview's current owner, has seen the old woman, in a gray bonnet and gown, hands folded in her lap, rocking patiently—as if she had all the time in the world.

The Hauntings
at the Surratt House

On the evening of April 14, 1865, Abraham Lincoln, president of the United States, was shot and killed by John Wilkes Booth while attending a performance at Ford's Theater in Washington, D.C. Less than three months later Mrs. Mary Surratt, an alleged co-conspirator in the assassination plot, was hanged along with three men also sentenced to death for their roles in the murder.

While stories of the late president's ghost wandering the corridors and rooms of the White House are relatively well known, less well known are the tales of Mrs. Surratt's ghost, said to frequent her old home and tavern in Surrattsville, Maryland. Located in southern Prince George's County about thirteen miles from Washington, Surrattsville is now known as Clinton. Mary Surratt's old home still stands on Brandywine Road, although it is now owned by the Maryland-National Capital Park and Planning Commission, which acquired the property in 1965.

Stories of odd events associated with the Surratt house first surfaced in the 1940s and 1950s when a widow lived in one half of the residence and rented out the other. People talked of having seen the ghost of Mrs. Surratt on the stairway between the first and second floors. Other people said that they heard men's voices in conversation at the back of the house when no one was there.

More recently, a man driving past the home spotted a gentleman dressed in old-fashioned black clothes walking up onto the front porch and into the house when it was closed to the public and there was presumably no reason for anyone to have been entering.

People inside the house have also witnessed unusual things. A guide giving a tour of the house had just moved her group from one upstairs bedroom to another when she sensed that she had left someone behind in the other room. When she went back to the first bedroom, she saw a girl in Victorian clothing straightening the bedspread and looking under the bed for something. At first, the guide assumed that the young girl belonged to the tour group and she started to walk away to find out who the girl's parents were. Then the guide was struck by the realization that the girl's appearance seemed odd and that there hadn't been any children in her tour group. When she looked back into the room, the child had disappeared. Another time, in the same bedroom, the teenage daughter of another guide saw the reflection, in the room's wall mirror, of a large man with a beard seated in a rocking chair. When the girl turned her head to look directly at him, the man vanished. Other people visiting the Surratt house have heard the sound of a child crying on the first floor or the sound of footsteps on the floor above.

Two women, Laurie Verge and Joan Chaconas, have probably spent more time in the Surratt house than anyone else. Laurie, who is park historian and museum manager for the Maryland-National Capital Park and Planning Commission, is in charge of activities at the Surratt house. Joan is current president of the Surratt Society, an organization dedicated to the preservation and interpretation of the Surratt home. Although both women say that they have always felt comfortable in the house, they have both experienced out-of-the-ordinary incidents. During the daytime, from her office on the second floor, Laurie has often heard the sound of steps in the hallway just outside her office. The steps sound like those made by a man in work boots walking from one end of the house to the other. Laurie and others have also heard footsteps on the second floor when they were downstairs in the part of the building that was

once a tavern. Many people, including Laurie, have smelled tobacco smoke throughout the house when no one was smoking. Joan, for her part, has seen the facial expression on a painting of Mary Surratt that hangs in one of the rooms seem to change at times from one of solemnity to one with a smile.

Who are the ghosts at the Surratt house and why are they there? If the shape seen by some people on the stairs was indeed that of Mary Surratt's ghost, has she returned because her soul is in torment over her part in the Lincoln assassination plot? Or is it because Mary Surratt was, as she claimed during her trial and as some continue to believe, innocent, and has therefore returned to protest the injustice done to her? And the sound of the man's footsteps and the scent of tobacco smoke—could these have been produced by the ghost of John Lloyd, the former policeman to whom Mrs. Surratt was renting her home and tavern at the time of Lincoln's death? Perhaps this haunting is connected with the fact that it was Lloyd's testimony which proved the most damning evidence against Mary Surratt. Could it have been that Lloyd lied and has been troubled for over a century by a guilty conscience?

While these questions may never be satisfactorily answered, anyone interested in finding out more about the ghosts at the Surratt house may visit the home themselves. Perhaps they will be able to experience firsthand some of the peculiar phenomena that so many others have reported.

The Disturbed Graves

Stories of modern development encroaching on areas best left to history are not rare in this day and age. Many historic homes have been razed to make way for new housing or their estates divided and sold in quarter-acre lots. In Talbot County, however, one development project did more than just disturb a historic area—it disturbed a ghost.

Mrs. Barrow lived with her husband and family on Indian Point Farm for eight years until they sold it in January 1987. Behind the house a short distance away was an unmarked graveyard that reportedly had been there for at least as long as the 150-year-old wood frame house. Although Mrs. Barrow recalls that odd things had been happening in her home since she had moved in, activity seemed to increase dramatically after the land there was converted for new house lots.

According to Mrs. Barrow, her family and neighbors had always known about the existence of the graveyard, and one woman had even said that a Captain Fairbanks had been buried there. Workers on the development project, however, inadvertently broke into three of the grave sites, uprooting pieces of a human skeleton. The bones, a skull and jawbone, were left on top of the earth until Mrs. Barrow's son noticed them and alerted his mother. She took pictures of the disturbed graves, including the areas where their brick-lined sections had been completely removed, and contacted the state's attorney. She was assured that the graves would be covered up, and they eventually were.

The story of the disturbed graves did not end there, however, for it was following this incident that the Barrow family began to suspect they were living with a ghost. Mrs. Barrow heard the sound of feet in bedroom slippers going down the stairs to the first floor several times in the middle of the night, though she knew that no one in her family was up and out of bed. One day a lamp she had turned on in the living room went off by itself as soon as she left the room. Mrs. Barrow could find nothing wrong with either the lamp or its bulb. Another time the dishwasher in the kitchen turned on by itself and she found herself talking to the invisible entity responsible for the action, telling it that she wasn't ready for the dishes to be washed. Still another time the fan over the electric range turned itself on while a kitchen tableful of surprised people started at hearing the unexpected noise. The sound of furniture being moved around in the two upstairs bedrooms became a frequent occurrence despite the fact that one room had wall-to-wall carpeting and no one was ever in either of the rooms when the sounds were being made.

Soon friends began to experience some of the phenomena. A friend of Mrs. Barrow who had always encouraged the ghost to show itself got the shock of her life one night when, she swears, someone tried to get into her bed. The woman told Mrs. Barrow that she watched the bed as it slowly became indented—as if someone were actually lying down on it. She also said that she got the strong feeling that it was a male rather than a female presence.

Mrs. Barrow also began to believe that her ghost was a man and, because she knew that Captain Fairbanks had been buried out behind her house, she began to think of it as the Captain. Once, when she became annoyed by the incessant sounds of furniture being moved around upstairs, she instructed her son-in-law to "go up and tell the Captain to cut it out." Good-naturedly, the son-in-law did as he was asked but got spooked when he went upstairs, found that he could follow the sound of slippered feet from room to room, and felt an unseen presence pass him.

Mrs. Barrow remembers her old ghost with a certain amount of fondness, for she credits him with having saved her family and home from what could have been a disastrous fire. At six o'clock one morning, she woke out of a very heavy sleep for no apparent reason, with the overwhelming thought that the house was on fire. However, there was no smoke to be seen or smelled. Mrs. Barrow nevertheless got out of bed to investigate. It was a very grateful homeowner who shortly after did locate a smoldering fire in the chimney and was able to put it out before any real harm was done.

Mount Airy's
Haunted Grounds

Located in Mount Airy, Howard County, the land that both Bill Johnson and Ed Small (not their real names) had their homes on had a variety of strange things linked to it. The sounds of laughter, people talking, and party music could be heard not infrequently in the evenings by all of the neighbors alongside the Johnson and Small properties. It was some time, however, before the residents came to accept the fact that they were living in a very unusual place.

Mr. Johnson's first encounter with the area's odd activities occurred when he was being shown an old wood frame farmhouse that he was interested in buying. Bill and the son of the owner were on the second floor, having just finished looking at the attic. The attic door was several feet away from where the two men had stopped to talk and Bill distinctly remembers having closed and locked it behind him. Without warning, the men's discussion was suddenly interrupted by the sound of the door slowly swinging open. Aware that there was no reason for the door to have suddenly opened on its own, Bill looked at his companion for some explanation. The owner's son shrugged his shoulders and said, "That just comes with the territory." No further mention of the incident was made and shortly thereafter Bill and his wife Carol decided to purchase the house, which is believed to have been built in the latter half of the nineteenth century.

The Johnsons' plans for their new home included extensive renovations that would make it larger and more comfortable to live in. One evening Bill and a friend were in the master bedroom at about eleven o'clock putting up drywall when they were startled to hear the agonizing sound of a woman's scream pierce the still air. Shaken, both men searched the house and grounds completely and could find nothing to account for the terrible scream. By mutual agreement they both decided to abandon their work for that particular evening and head home.

Strange things continued to happen after most of the repairs had been completed and the Johnsons moved in. Footsteps could be heard either coming down the stairs from the second floor or along the floorboards in the attic. Bill scoured the attic for signs of squirrels or other animals but couldn't find anything. One night he awoke from a sound sleep to find a "Casparlike" form about four to five feet tall standing in front of the bedroom closet. He chose not to wake his wife and instead watched the form until it slowly faded away about ten minutes later. At other times, Bill would hear the sound of a baby crying down the hall from the master bedroom. Once he happened to walk through the family room during the day and evidently disturbed something that had been sitting in the rocking chair, for it was swaying back and forth as though someone had just gotten up from it. Another time the Johnsons' rather timid dog—not a frequent barker—rushed barking to the part of the house Bill was in and led him to the doorway of the family room, where he sat down and refused to go farther. Bill could see that the rocking chair was moving back and forth, as though there were someone sitting in it, and he convinced the dog to approach the chair with him. When the two reached the chair it stopped moving and the dog seemed to look in the air at something walking out of the room.

Ghosts & Haunted Houses of Maryland

The Johnsons and a later addition to their family, a daughter, have remained in their home despite the unexplainable things they've witnessed because they've always felt that the presence was a friendly one. Things still continue to happen, however. A picture taken of Bill and Carol standing in front of the house showed an odd cloudlike formation between them when it was developed. Several weeks later, the cloud seemed to fade away as though it had never been there. More recently, Carol has seen the same ghostly form that her husband saw thirteen years ago. Occasionally, the Johnsons can hear the sounds of violin music and laughter coming from the property once owned by their neighbor Ed Small.

Ed Small, who no longer lives in Mount Airy, had a new house built in 1981 on the property adjoining the Johnsons'. The land had all once belonged to the farmhouse, and off to one side of Bill and Carol's house, in the middle of a cornfield, is the old family cemetery plot.

Ed didn't notice anything particularly unusual about his new home until he went to put in a garden the spring after he'd moved in. As he was digging, he unearthed a small metal tag surrounded by bits of old wood. The tag had the word "nigra" hammered into it. Curious, Ed pocketed the tag and later brought it into the house, where he placed it on the fireplace mantel. Several days later, he began to hear violin music and voices coming from the area where he'd put in his garden, but there was never anything out there when he went to investigate. He and other neighbors could hear the sounds almost every night.

Within a month after Ed had dug his garden and brought the tag into the house, he began to hear footsteps walking up and down the stairs in his home and the sound of a door constantly being opened and closed.

After having been told about the tag, Bill Johnson undertook some research and discovered two very interesting things. First, slaves buried in the nineteenth century in Maryland were often buried in wooden coffins with small metal identifying tags affixed to them. The word "nigra" meant negro. Secondly, according to information in land records about the old farm property, the location Ed had unwittingly chosen for his garden was probably the area that had been used to bury slaves.

Shortly after learning this, Ed decided to return the tag to its original place and abandon his garden. After that, nothing unusual happened again in his home.

The Voices
at Point Lookout

Located at the southern tip of St. Mary's County on a low peninsula where the Potomac and Chesapeake meet, Point Lookout State Park is a popular recreation spot for thousands of Marylanders each summer. It's hard to believe that it was once a camp for Confederate prisoners of war and that almost 4,000 of those prisoners died there. It's even harder to believe that some of those men are said to still make their presence known at the last place they lived on earth.

The area known as Point Lookout had its beginnings in the midnineteenth century as a bayside resort. When the Civil War broke out, its owner was experiencing financial difficulties and the approximately 400 acres of land were eventually sold to the U.S. government as a site for a military hospital. The Hammond General Hospital was soon erected, but it was not long before the government decided that the area could also be used as a prisoner of war depot.

Officially known as Camp Hoffman, the camp never had barracks—prisoners used small tents. The low, marshy land was not beneficial to the health of its inhabitants and many men lost their lives to smallpox, dysentery, and scurvy. Between July 1863 and June 1865, over 50,000 Confederate soldiers passed through the camp. A year after the war ended, Camp Hoffman was dismantled.

The Voices at Point Lookout

Two monuments were later erected at Point Lookout, one by the state and one by the federal government, in memory of the many men who died there. In 1964 the land was purchased by the state of Maryland for conversion to a recreational area, and tales of tortured souls wandering the grounds of Point Lookout began to circulate soon after it was opened to the public.

One former park manager, Gerald Sword, had a most interesting and vivid exposure to the area's hauntings as a result of his stay at the lighthouse there in the 1970s. According to accounts by Sword, he began to hear noises in various parts of the large, twenty-room house only a few months after he had moved in. The sounds of doors opening and closing, footsteps, and crashing objects became frequent but provided no clues to their source. Soon Sword also began to notice the sound of voices in the house and could even faintly hear some conversations, but he could never pinpoint just exactly where they were coming from. On one occasion, he believed that he witnessed six separate invisible entities walk into his house right past where he was standing—he experienced an unnerving sensation of air currents rushing past him while the other air around him was still. At other times he heard the sound of someone snoring coming from somewhere behind the cupboards in the kitchen, but he was never able to find anything to account for it. One night, while seated in his kitchen, Sword got the uncanny feeling that he was being watched. Getting up from his seat, he walked to the door and peered through the window. He immediately saw the face of a young man wearing a floppy cap and a sack coat looking back at him through the window. Stunned, Sword grabbed for the door to throw it open, only to see the man on the other side walk away and disappear through the screens of the enclosed porch.

Among all of his many and varied experiences at Point Lookout, this latter incident was one Sword was able to research. He found out that in 1878 a severe storm had caused the breakup of a large steamer just north of the point. Thirty-one people, including a young crewman by the name of Joseph Haney, drowned in the accident. A newspaper description of Haney, whose body was washed up and buried near the point, tallied exactly with the features and clothes of the young man Sword had seen on his porch.

There are other stories about Point Lookout State Park, including accounts of another haunted house, St. Michael's Manor. Built in 1805 and located across from the Confederate monument, the home has had many owners who experienced abnormal incidents. Ghostly happenings have also been reported to have taken place in the camp areas and along the roadsides of the park.

Perhaps the most fascinating aspect of the hauntings at Point Lookout was revealed by a paranormal investigation conducted by a team that included the famous ghost hunter Hans Holzer. Using tape recorders, the group was able to collect recordings of mysterious voices in the lighthouse and on the grounds of the park through a procedure known as electronic voice phenomenon, or EVP. This curious technique involves voices that can be heard on a tape although nothing was audible during the recording process. EVP has never been satisfactorily explained. Voices on the tapes recorded by the investigating group at Point Lookout belonged to both men and women. One recording had the distinct sound of a steamboat whistle on it, although steamboats operating in the area are a thing of long ago. Men's voices on the recordings utter such phrases as "living in the lighthouse," "my home," and "fire if they get too close to you." One woman's voice was recorded as saying the word "vaccine." Yet another woman's voice was heard on a tape saying, "Let us not take any objections to what they are doing."

Explanations? EVP is still little understood, although if one were to believe that the voices belonged to entities at the park, one would have to assume that there are indeed a number of ghosts in the area—certainly an interesting addition to what Point Lookout State Park already has to offer visitors.

The Ghost
and the Dining Room Table

When Diane Glover bought the old English mahogany table from an antique shop in Funkstown, little did she suspect that the table came with its own ghost. Six years and two house moves later, Diane now recognizes that the strange events that began to happen in her home were the result of antics carried out by a spirit who had decided to become the table's traveling companion.

Carol Engstrom, owner of Chaney House and its co-located antique shop, a magnificent brick building built around 1840 in downtown Funkstown, Washington County, knew that there had been stories of a ghost in the house. In fact, before Mrs. Engstrom's family purchased Chaney House in 1942, the previous owners said that there was a ghost and admitted to having heard mysterious piano playing at night. Carol, who had never herself noticed any paranormal activity in her home, remembers that a housekeeper for the family claimed to have actually encountered the ghost. The woman had been working at the kitchen sink when she suddenly had a feeling that someone was standing behind her. Turning around, she saw a woman before her who wore an apron over a dark, old-fashioned dress. The woman's dark hair was pulled back into a bun at the base of her head. As inexplicably as the mysterious apparition had materialized, she vanished into the air as the incredulous housekeeper watched. No other members of the household ever saw the woman appear again.

Diane Glover of Reno, Nevada, had been looking for just the right antique table for her dining room when, in 1981 she heard from a friend living in Funkstown of a table that seemed perfect. Sight unseen, the table was purchased by Diane from Carol Engstrom's antique shop and shipped to Reno.

The first spooky incident that Diane recalls happened not long after the arrival of the table when she was on the first level of her trilevel home reading the newspaper with her two dogs at her feet. Her husband John, a physician, was at the hospital. Diane noticed the sound of footsteps above her, walking up and down the hall. Aware that she was the only person home, she cautiously ventured upstairs with the two dogs to investigate. Upon arriving in the hallway where she thought the sounds had originated, she was unable to find anything to account for them, although she was struck by the odd behavior of her dogs—both were wagging their tails and acting as though a great friend of theirs was present. Diane returned downstairs to resume her reading. Soon she heard the footsteps again. This time she went to the upstairs hall with a poker in one hand, convinced that there was an intruder in her home. Once again, a search of the house provided no clues. Although the sound of someone walking around upstairs happened once more after she had returned to her reading, Diane found no one when she went back up to investigate.

Three months later, the Glovers moved to Phoenix and with them went their beautiful dining room table. Diane took the precaution of removing the brass clips from the table and packing them carefully with her silver so that they could be hand-carried to the new house. When she arrived in Phoenix and unpacked her silver, the clips were missing. Although she searched thoroughly, she could not find the clips and could not understand how they could have been lost when she had packed and carried them herself.

Other odd things began to happen. John Glover's bathrobe disappeared from where it usually hung on a hook on the back of a bathroom door. Two weeks later, the robe reappeared on the hook. A particularly squeaky kitchen door connected the garage to the house; alone at night waiting for her husband to come home, Diane would often hear the door opening and closing, although she could never discover any reason for the sound and always found the door locked when she went into the room to check it. John also witnessed this phenomenon one evening when he went to the kitchen to investigate after he and Diane heard the door slam four or five times.

Diane, meanwhile, began to think that all of the odd things happening in her house might be understandable if she were to consider the idea that she had a ghost. Deciding that a ghost did provide an explanation, she nicknamed it "Sadie," and even jokingly asked it to return the brass clips that had never been found. The next day, while checking her silver, Diane found the clips right where she had put them for the move.

Other unusual activity began to occur. Diane would occasionally hear a whispering sound, as if someone were talking to her. Other times she thought she noticed a flicker out of the corner of her eye. Finally, one night she became convinced of a supernatural presence in her home when she walked through what she described as "a strange mist" as she was passing from one room to another. Immediately, she sensed that it was Sadie and she received a picture in her mind's eye of a woman in her forties or fifties, her hair in a bun, wearing a gray- green dress of a coarse material with an apron over the front of it. Diane also got the impression that, whoever it was, it was a friendly presence.

Sometime later, Diane began to wonder how a ghost could have been in both of the houses she and her husband had lived in. The only thing that coincided with the onset of ghostly activity had been the acquisition of the antique table. Soon Diane was in touch with Carol Engstrom. Since Diane's description of her ghost so closely resembled the one that the housekeeper had given of the ghost at Chaney House, the two women agreed that the ghosts were one and the same. Evidently, Sadie has some emotional attachment to the table and has decided to go wherever it goes, although no one is sure why she has chosen to do this. Carol theorizes that Sadie could have been a nurse who worked at Chaney House at one period during the Civil War when it was converted to a hospital. The table, in fact, had sat for over a year in the front part of the house where operations on wounded soldiers were believed to have taken place.

Sadie, for her part, doesn't seem anxious to explain why she has a connection to the table, although she has gone to some lengths to convince nonbelievers of her existence. Diane recalls one occasion when a visiting friend was discussing, in the Glover kitchen one morning, the improbability of Sadie's existence. Breakfast had just ended and the dishes, with cantaloupe halves in them, were on the kitchen counter. At one of the remarks of the friend, a cantaloupe suddenly turned itself over in its dish. Everyone in the kitchen, including the cynical friend—who lost a great deal of his cynicism that morning—saw the remarkable cantaloupe flip. More recently, when the Glovers moved to another house in Phoenix in December 1986, some moving men were given their own demonstration of Sadie's antics as they watched a radio tuning dial move itself from station to station; one man who had made pointed remarks about the nonexistence of ghosts had his jacket temporarily "misplaced" by Sadie.

Diane has become very accustomed to Sadie and no longer finds herself disturbed at the majority of the ghost's mischievous pranks. Household objects disappear and reappear all the time at Sadie's whim. However, one of Sadie's jokes that Diane felt was strongly lacking in humor was the disappearance of the Glovers' luggage just before they were supposed to go on a trip. Diane and John were forced to purchase new luggage after a search of their home proved fruitless. The day after the new suitcases were brought into the house, the Glovers found their old ones—right in the closet where they belonged. Sadie was given a sound lecture on the value of money after that episode.